# TRANSECTS

## 100 YEARS

OF LANDSCAPE ARCHITECTURE AND REGIONAL PLANNING
AT THE SCHOOL OF DESIGN
OF THE UNIVERSITY OF PENNSYLVANIA

**RICHARD WELLER AND MEGHAN TALAROWSKI**

Published by:
Applied Research + Design Publishing
Gordon Goff: Publisher
www.appliedresearchanddesign.com
info@appliedresearchanddesign.com

Copyright © 2014 by Applied Research + Design Publishing
ISBN: 978-1-941806-29-6
10 09 08 07 06 5 4 3 2 1  First Edition

Graphic Design: Meghan Talarowski
Edited by: Richard Weller and Meghan Talarowski
Color Separations and Printing: ORO Group Ltd.
Printed in China.

This book was printed and bound using a variety of sustainable manufacturing processes and materials including VOC- and formaldehyde-free glues, and phthalate-free laminations. The text is printed using offset sheetfed lithographic printing process in 4 color on 157gsm premium matt art paper.

Applied Research + Design Publishing makes a continuous effort to minimize the overall carbon footprint of its publications. As part of this goal, Applied Research + Design Publishing, in association with Global ReLeaf, arranges to plant trees to replace those used in the manufacturing of the paper produced for its books. Global ReLeaf is an international campaign run by American Forests, one of the world's oldest nonprofit conservation organizations. Global ReLeaf is American Forests' education and action program that helps individuals, organizations, agencies, and corporations improve the local and global environment by planting and caring for trees.

Library of Congress data: available upon request

For information on our distribution, please visit our website
www.appliedresearchanddesignpublishing.com

## ACKNOWLEDGEMENTS

We wish to thank all the alumni who responded to our requests for background information and personal stories. We also wish to thank the current landscape faculty and other Penn alumni in academia and professional practice who responded to interview questions.

Thank you to previous chairs James Corner and John Dixon Hunt for their input. We are particularly grateful to former chair Anne Whiston Spirn, who spent considerable time fleshing out several decades and locating images; Laurie Olin, who entertained us with countless stories and provided such a depth of knowledge regarding the school; and Carol McHarg, who opened her home and personal records to us on more than one occasion.

Thanks also go to the senior representatives from the offices of OLIN, Wallace Roberts Todd (WRT) and Andropogon, who took the time to meet with us and supply information.

This book would not have been possible without the especially generous guidance of Bill Whitaker and Nancy Thorne in the Architectural Archives of the University of Pennsylvania. Erin McCabe was a great help getting us started in our search for the program's first graduates; Barrett Doherty was instrumental in providing iconic imagery of the school; and as usual, in all matters administrative, Diane Pringle and Darcy Van Buskirk were irreplaceable. For editing assistance, we are grateful to Dr. Tatum Hands, Matthew Wiener and Claire Hoch.

As a guide to the history of the school, "The Book of the School" by Ann L. Strong and George E. Thomas was an invaluable resource, as was "Peter Shepheard" by Annabel Downs.

Finally, we would like to acknowledge the enthusiastic support of Dean Marilyn Jordan Taylor and PennDesign's promotions team; Rick Fitzgerald, Megan Schmidgal and Janhavi Chandra.

James Corner and
Marilyn Jordan Taylor

# FOREWORD

## Marilyn Jordan Taylor
Dean, School of Design, University of Pennsylvania

As you stroll through the words and images of this remarkable short history, I hope that you will be mindful of the future of landscape architecture even as you are enjoying a fresh look at its past. Leafing through these pages you will find resonant stories, lasting friends and legacy figures sharing moments of brilliance interwoven with periods of change, particularly during the sixty years since Dean G. Holmes Perkins reached out to Professor Ian McHarg to create an ecology-defined program in landscape architecture at PennDesign.

Perkins' prescient vision of design at Penn was broad and cross-disciplinary; the breadth and depth of cross-disciplinary thinking that characterizes our school today flows from the formidable steps he took as dean. McHarg invented a program that was to engage and inspire landscape architects, architects, ecologists, urbanists and regional planners for decades. At Penn, he found himself among faculty colleagues in architecture, city planning, history and the fine arts who shared his penchant for dialog and argument, for commitment and risk—all to the enduring benefit of PennDesign students and our school.

Leadership in the design academy is a challenging and changing endeavor. McHarg was followed by Anne Whiston Spirn, John Dixon Hunt, James Corner and now Richard Weller, each extending the definition, influence and experience of landscape architecture, individually and collectively. The faculty, students and alumni of the landscape programs and initiatives at Penn have declared the importance of identifying and cultivating a discipline, separate from architecture, of landscape architecture. They have articulated and demonstrated why we must design with, rather than in spite of, nature. They have welded a cross-disciplinary design approach in which the building is but another element of the landscape, and sometimes indistinguishable from it. They offer designs through which culture and experience extend materiality and sensuality to an experience of pleasure and beauty. Their perception and passion bring timely focus to the urban condition, the nature of the city and the contribution of landscape in healing the physical and philosophical distance of urbanized places and informal settlements from their natural settings. They created the field of landscape urbanism and continue to extend its potential. They hold the keys to the broadest definition of human and physical resilience in the face of extreme weather. They see the need to extend their skill to address the challenge of protecting and defending the biodiversity that gives us life.

And so begins the next exciting 100 years of landscape architecture at PennDesign.

# INTRODUCTION

## Richard Weller

Martin and Margy Meyerson Chair of Urbanism and Professor and Chair of the Department of Landscape Architecture at the University of Pennsylvania

This book commemorates 100 years of Landscape Architecture and Regional Planning at the University of Pennsylvania. Landscape architecture was first introduced as a subject in the School of Fine Arts (now the School of Design) in 1914 through a series of lectures by George Burnap, landscape architect for the United States Capitol. It is from these lectures that we have measured our first centenary.

The B.L.A. program was officially introduced at Penn in 1924 under the direction of Robert Wheelwright, a founding member of the American Society of Landscape Architects. The program graduated 23 landscape architects before its wartime suspension in 1942. Although no degrees were conferred, occasional courses in landscape architecture continued to be taught at Penn over the next decade before a new Dean, G. Holmes Perkins, recruited Ian McHarg to revive the landscape architecture program in 1954.

In 1957, McHarg became chair of the new Department of Landscape Architecture offering a B.L.A., as well as a one-year M.L.A. for architects. In 1965, a large grant from the Ford Foundation enabled McHarg to found a new regional planning program and to assemble a faculty versed in natural sciences. While enrollments in landscape architecture remained stable during the 1970s, enrollments in the regional planning program soared and this necessarily shaped faculty tenure appointments. With the publication of his manifesto "Design With Nature" in 1969, McHarg became an internationally renowned leader in ecological landscape planning and received a National Medal of Arts from President George H.W. Bush. Although the profession increasingly found most of its work at a civic scale, McHarg's description of the landscape architect as a 'steward of the earth' is to this day the discipline's most powerful and compelling *raison d'etre*.

By 1985, however, with changes in governmental policies and reduced funding for environmental programs, the enrollment in regional planning was reduced to 2–3 students per year. In the academy, waves of new theory and experimental modes of representation found their way from architecture into landscape architecture and challenged the authority of large scale planning based on objective mapping.

In 1986, Penn alum Anne Whiston Spirn was recruited to succeed McHarg as chair with the mandate of extending the department's legacy and renewing its commitment to design. The challenge was to reshape the full-time faculty in order to teach landscape architects, now the vast majority of students in the department, and to rebuild the regional planning program in collaboration with the Department of City and Regional Planning. Through her writings and community engagement, Spirn continued McHarg's grand vision of an ecologically healthier world but orientated the program toward the cultural milieu of the urban environment. Spirn's book "The Granite Garden" (1984) was a prescient survey of urban ecology, one that would find consolidation in the movement of landscape urbanism emanating from Penn over a decade later. In 2001, Spirn was awarded the prestigious International Cosmos Prize for what continues to be a career devoted to compressing the gap between the art, science and sociology of ecological design.

Spirn was succeeded as chair in 1994 by garden historian John Dixon Hunt. Hunt brought a new level of historical and theoretical rigor to the program and launched Penn Studies in Landscape Architecture, an internationally recognized publication series on landscape history and design. Since his appointment, Hunt has written a consistent stream of high quality works of landscape architectural history, confirming his reputation as the world's pre-eminent landscape historian. Hunt was able to connect history to contemporary landscape architecture, providing it with the roots it needed.

Continuing what Spirn had begun, Hunt oversaw a design renaissance at Penn as faculty such as Anuradha Mathur and James Corner were able to consolidate a culture of design experimentation throughout the program. Corner's wide ranging writings emphasized design's capacity to catalyze social and ecological change and his edited volume "Recovering Landscape: Essays in Contemporary Landscape Theory" (1996) became synonymous with a discipline on the ascendant. Mathur and her partner Dilip da Cunha drew on post-colonial and post-structural theory, arguing through exhibitions and publications for the importance of how landscape is conceptualized, before it is designed.

In 2000, Corner was named the new chair of the Department. Over the course of the next decade, Corner amassed a strong design faculty and developed a culture of creative and competitive individualism. Along with other Penn alumni such as Charles Waldheim and Chris Reed, Corner established the principles of a new school of thought known as landscape urbanism that propelled landscape architecture to the forefront of debates about contemporary urban design. Corner's commitment to testing ideas and techniques through design application, followed by the spectacular success of his firm, James Corner Field Operations, ensured landscape architecture at Penn was looked to as the world's leading design program. In 2010, James Corner Field Operations received the National Landscape Design Award from the Smithsonian's Cooper-Hewitt National Design Museum. In the same year, Penn was awarded the prize for world's best landscape architecture program at the European Biennial of Landscape Architecture in Barcelona.

In 2013, I accepted the position as the sixth chair of landscape architecture at Penn. The history of the school, described in this book, represents an important legacy and I am excited to be involved in shaping this legacy into the future. Where some see only polarizations between McHarg, Spirn, Hunt and Corner, I see the essential coordinates of what it now means to be a landscape architect in the 21st century. Through their work and that of the department they have led, we find exemplary vision, method, depth and technique working across all scales.

The question now is how to take that which we have learned from their work and educate a new generation of landscape architects: a generation who will not only continue to lead the discipline, but more importantly influence the world beyond—radically, profoundly and beautifully. The answer to this question lies in all the things that make a great school. It lies in how closely ancillary studies in history, theory, media, materials and ecology are linked to the design studio. It lies in how actively we enable interdisciplinary connections and opportunities. It lies in the flow of ideas that move through the school and the proximity of students and faculty. It lies in our propensity for intellectual and creative experimentation. It lies in how we apply design intelligence to the complex systemic issues that will dominate 21st century life. It lies in how we build a globally relevant research platform. And all of this relates back to the way we value and critically interpret the legacy of this school.

*****

This book has been researched, written and designed in collaboration with Meghan Talarowski whose exceptional capacity for clear thinking, organizational skills, good humor and attention to detail have made this book possible. We don't claim it to be a definitive history, but it does attempt to capture a representative picture of the school. It also contains many interesting anecdotes from former students as well as some wonderful items from the archives, such as Ian McHarg's scribbles on a napkin, and quotes from James Corner's studio syllabi. These seemed to us to say far more than we could in words.

Penn has always been chaired by leaders in the field with big personalities, but a chair is nothing without good faculty. There have been many brilliant teachers and selfless administrators who have made the program's reputation, and you will find their names at the end of this volume. There is also a list of the alumni and landmark moments in design history and culture more broadly.

The book is organized into 10-year increments. The final chapter, "The Future" features a diverse collection of statements from current and past faculty, and from prominent alumni, about their teaching methods and their research directions. This stands testament to Penn as an incubator of design intelligence.

And finally, in the background of all this, since 1974 when he first came to teach at Penn, has been Laurie Olin. Not only has he led one of the world's most respected practices, but he has consistently taught inspirational design studios and drawing classes emphasizing the art and craft of landscape architecture. In 2013, Laurie received the National Medal of Arts, an accolade given to only three landscape architects (Lawrence Halprin, Dan Kiley and Ian McHarg) before him.

As Laurie said to us over a bottle of wine in a café in downtown Philadelphia, while we were researching this book, "We have a bad building, no money and never enough time ... but we have ideas and we have good people. Penn has always had good people."

花の万博記念
「コスモス国際賞」
International Cosmos Prize for 2001

Ian McHarg receiving
the National Medal of
Arts, Anne Whiston
Spirn receiving the
International
Cosmos Prize

1990, 2001

James Corner receiving
the National Landscape
Design Award, Laurie
Olin receiving the
National Medal of Arts

2010, 2013

# CONTENTS

1914-1923
PAGES 16-21

1924-1933
PAGES 22-31

1934-1943
PAGES 32-41

1944-1953
PAGES 42-49

1954-1963
PAGES 50-61

1964-1973
PAGES 62-97

1974-1983
PAGES 98-113

1984-1993
PAGES 114-139

1994-2003
PAGES 140-169

2004-2013
PAGES 170-205

future
PAGES 206-250

Landscape architecture was a young profession in the early years of the 20th century. Established by Olmsted in the later part of the 19th century and introduced to America at large at the 1893 World's Columbian Exposition, there were still few trained professionals when Penn first began its forays into the field. Not yet ready to commit to a full program in the training of landscape architects, the School of Fine Arts nonetheless acknowledged the importance of this new professional movement by hosting a series of lectures on the topic in 1914 and 1918 by George Burnap and Jacques Gréber.

# 1914-1923

Ten part lecture series in Landscape Design by George Burnap

Lecture series on the Philadelphia Parkway by Jacques Gréber

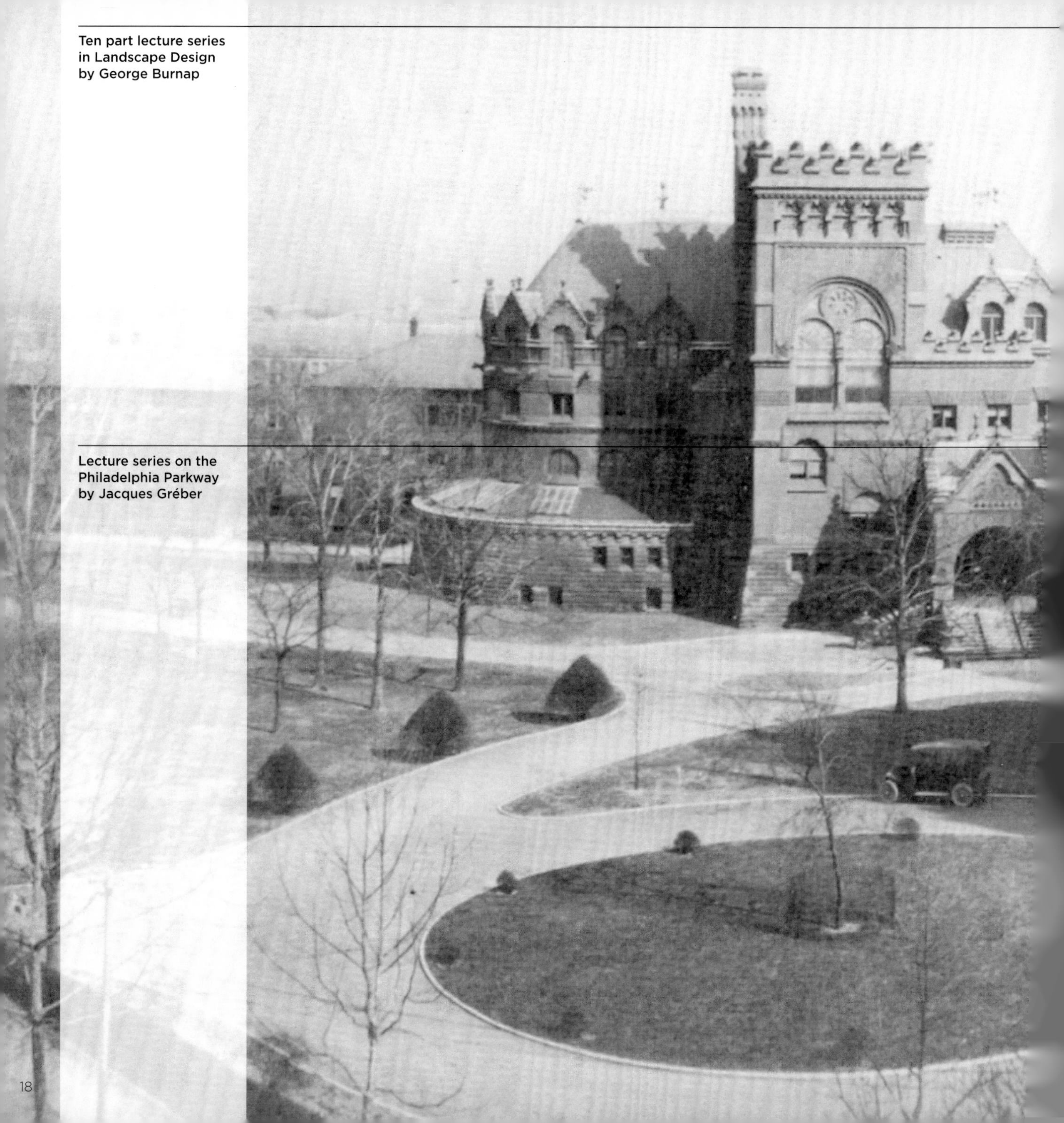

| | |
|---|---|
| **World War I Begins**<br>Corbusier's Dom-ino<br>Gaudi's Guell Park | 1914 |
| **Ford produces 1 millionth car**<br>**First transcontinental telephone call**<br>Einstein's "General Theory of Relativity"<br>Geddes' "Cities in Evolution" | 1915 |
| **US National Park Service established**<br>**First Federal Highway Act in US**<br>Dada begins in Zurich<br>Jensen's Columbus Park | 1916 |
| **Russian Revolution**<br>**US enters World War I**<br>Duchamp's "Fountain"<br>Freud's "Introduction to Psychoanalysis"<br>American Institute of City Planners founded | 1917 |
| **World War I ends** | 1918 |
| **Prohibition begins**<br>**Acadia and Grand Canyon**<br>**National Parks established**<br>Bauhaus founded | 1919 |
| **Warren G. Harding elected US President**<br>**US women given right to vote**<br>**Cordona perfects triple somersault** | 1920 |
| Farrand's Dumbarton Oaks | 1921 |
| Robert Moses begins NYC career | 1922 |
| **Calvin Coolidge, US Vice President,**<br>**assumes presidency on Harding's death**<br>Harvard offers Master in City Planning | 1923 |

College Green,
early 1900s

Ten part lecture series in Landscape Design, taught by George Burnap

Housing and Town Planning, ten lectures, by Dr. Carol Aronovici, Philadelphia.

The Decorative Element in Architecture, one lecture, by William Francklyn Paris, New York City.

Landscape Design, ten lectures, by George Burnap, Washington, D. C.

## ASTRONOMY.

ASTRONOMY 1. *Elementary Astronomy.*—Young's *Lessons in Astronomy.* Two hours. First term. One unit. ASSISTANT PROFESSOR BARTON.

ASTRONOMY 2. *Astronomy.*—Young's *Manual of Astronomy.* Prerequisites, Mathematics 1 and 2. Three hours. First term. One and a half units. PROFESSOR DOOLITTLE and ASSISTANT PROFESSOR BARTON.

ASTRONOMY 3. *Practical Astronomy.*—Doolittle's *Practical Astronomy.* Prerequisites, Mathematics 7 and 9. Three hours. Second term. One and a half units. PROFESSOR DOOLITTLE.

ASTRONOMY 4. *Practical Astronomy.*—Continuation of 3. Prerequisite, Astronomy 3. Three hours. Both terms. Three units. PROFESSOR DOOLITTLE.

ASTRONOMY 5.* *Theoretical Astronomy.*—Watson's *Theoretical Astronomy* and Oppolzer's *Lehrbuch zur Bahnbestimmung,* Vol. I. Prerequisites, Astronomy 2 and Mathematics 7 and 9. A reading knowledge of French and German is desirable. Three hours. Both terms. Three units. ASSISTANT PROFESSOR BARTON.

ASTRONOMY 6. *Least Squares and Geodesy.*—Crandall's *Text-book on Geodesy and Least Squares.* Prerequisites, Mathematics 7 and 9. Two hours. Second term. One unit. PROFESSOR DOOLITTLE.

## BACTERIOLOGY.

BACTERIOLOGY 1. *Elementary Bacteriology.*—First year bacteriology of the course in Medicine. Elective in Arts and Science and the four year course in Biology. One hour lecture throughout the first term and fourteen hours laboratory second term. Four units. PROFESSOR ABBOTT, ASSISTANT PROFESSOR BERGEY, DR. SMYTH, DR. STEWART.

BACTERIOLOGY 2. *Advanced Bacteriology.*—Individual work by advanced students in any field of purely scientific or applied bacteriology. Prerequisite, Bacteriology 1. Hours to be arranged. Both terms. PROFESSOR ABBOTT, ASSISTANT PROFESSOR BERGEY.

* Primarily for graduate students.

George Burnap and
Jacques Gréber

1918

By 1924, the School of Fine Arts was committed to formally training landscape architects. Robert Wheelwright, a founding member of the American Society of Landscape Architects, as well as a prominent landscape architect working in New York, was invited to chair the newly established department of undergraduates. The program grew swiftly, from Wheelwright alone teaching three students in 1924 to a peak of three professors teaching 22 students in 1929. Unfortunately, the stock market crash and The Depression severely dampened the prospects of the program throughout the 1930s, causing a sharp drop in student enrollment and forcing Wheelwright to reduce staff.

# 1924-1933

Landscape architecture program established, five year Bachelor of Landscape Architecture (B.L.A.) degree offered

First landscape architecture graduate, Edith Crosby Stuart neé Brown, B.L.A. '30

| | |
|---|---|
| Calvin Coolidge elected US President<br>Ford produces ten millionth car<br>Hilbersheimer's "Study for an Ideal City"<br>Mumford's "Sticks and Stones"<br>Martinetti's "Futurism and Fascism" | 1924 |
| International Expo in Paris<br>Bauhaus moves to Dessau | 1925 |
| NBC established, first major US<br>broadcast network | 1926 |
| Charles Lindbergh makes first<br>trans-Atlantic flight<br>The Jazz Singer, first "talkie" or motion<br>picture with sound, released | 1927 |
| Herbert Hoover elected US President<br>Amelia Earhart makes first solo female<br>trans-Atlantic flight<br>Internationaux d'architecture moderne<br>(CIAM) founded<br>Green's Green Gables | 1928 |
| Wall Street crash<br>St. Valentine's Day massacre in Chicago<br>Mies van der Rohe's Barcelona Pavillion<br>Wright and Stein's Radburn NJ plan<br>Harvard starts first US city planning school | 1929 |
| Great Depression begins<br>Pluto is discovered | 1930 |
| World car production reaches 31 million<br>Corbusier's Villa Savoye<br>Lamb's Empire State Building, world's<br>tallest building (until 1954) | 1931 |
| Franklin D. Roosevelt elected<br>US President<br>Wright's "Disappearing City"<br>Calder first exhibits "stabiles"<br>and "mobiles" | 1932 |
| Prohibition repealed<br>New Deal established<br>Joyce's "Ulysses" allowed in US<br>Bauhaus closes | 1933 |

Early design studio

In a letter to the New York Times in 1924, Robert Wheelwright wrote:

"There is but one profession whose main objective has been to co-ordinate the works of man with preexistent nature and that is landscape architecture. The complexity of the problems which the landscape architect is called upon to solve, involving a knowledge of engineering, architecture, soils, plant materials, ecology, etc., combined with aesthetic appreciation can hardly be expected of a person who is not highly trained and who does not possess a degree of culture."

## THE DEPARTMENT OF LANDSCAPE ARCHITECTURE

ANNOUNCEMENT.—The urgent demand upon the University of Pennsylvania for a course in Landscape Architecture has led the Trustees to establish this work, to be opened in September, 1924, with an educational standard, teaching personnel and equipment which will place it at full level with the course in Architecture. The new course is framed on the conception that Landscape Architecture is a fine art and it will comprise a range of studies, both technical and cultural, deemed necessary to a thorough preparation for the general practice of this art, while the organization of the course is such that ultimately will permit the development of instruction in city planning. As an earnest of the aims and standards of the work the Trustees have placed it under the direction of Robert Wheelwright, Landscape Architect and Member of the American Society of Landscape Architects. A graduate of Harvard University (A.B., 1906, and Master of Landscape Architecture, 1908), Professor Wheelwright has achieved success as a practitioner in this field, both in New York and Philadelphia, while, as member of the American Society of Landscape Architects, he was one of the founders and for ten years an editor of its official organ, Landscape Architecture.

The new course and its general and special advantages are described below.

### THE COURSE IN LANDSCAPE ARCHITECTURE

It is believed that in establishing this course the University will meet a growing demand throughout the country and thus fulfill a need of the community. Landscape Architecture, still young as a profession, has advanced so rapidly in this country that to-day the United States leads the world in this art, offering more and better opportunities for its study, and for practice, than any other country.

# COURSE IN LANDSCAPE ARCHITECTURE

## FIRST YEAR—FRESHMAN

| Subject and Number of Course | Units 1st Term | 2d Term |
|---|---|---|
| L.A. 41: History of L.A...... | 1.5 | 1.5 |
| L.A. 20: El. of Plant Struct... | .. | 1 |
| L.A. 26: L.A. Drawing........ | 0.5 | .. |
| Arch. 26: Architecture........ | 1 | 1 |
| Arch. 10: Elm. of Arch....... | 1 | 1 |
| Arch. 11: Freehand Draw. I... | 1 | .. |
| Arch. 12: Freehand Draw. II.. | .. | 1 |
| F.A. 27: Projections, Sh. and Sh., Perspective........ | 1.5 | 1.5 |
| Totals.................... | 6.5 | 7 |
| Professional Units.......... | 13.5 | |
| Eng. 1: Composition.......... | 1 | 1 |
| Eng. 40: Literature.......... | 1 | .. |
| Fr. 2: Reading and Comp.*... | 1.5 | 1.5 |
| Math. 2: Plane Trig......... | .. | 1.5 |
| P.E. 1: Physical Education or M.T. 1: Military Training | 0.5 | 0.5 |
| Totals.................... | 4 | 4.5 |
| Non-Professional Units...... | 8.5 | |
| Toral, First-Year Units...... | 22 | |

## SECOND YEAR—SOPHOMORE

| Subject and Number of Course | Units 1st Term | 2d Term |
|---|---|---|
| L.A. 42: Theory and App..... | 1 | 1 |
| L.A. 1: Arch. Design......... | 2.5 | 2.5 |
| L.A. 21 or 22: Plant Mat.†... | 2 | 2 |
| Arch. 13: Freehand Draw. III. | 1 | 1 |
| C.E. 169: Surveying.......... | 1.5 | 0.5 |
| Totals.................... | 8 | 7 |
| Professional Units.......... | 15 | |
| F.A. 2: Arch. History‡........ | | |
| Eng. 3: Composition.......... | 1 | 1 |
| Fr. 4: Reading and Comp.*... | .. | 1 |
| P.E. 2: Physical Education or M.T. 2: Military Training | 1.5 0.5 | 1.5 0.5 |
| Totals.................... | | |
| Non-Professional Units...... | 3 | 4 |
| Total, Second-Year Units.... | 7 | |
| | 22 | |

## THIRD YEAR—JUNIOR

| Subject and Number of Course | Units 1st Term | 2d Term |
|---|---|---|
| L.A. 2: Design, Class C...... | 4 | 4 |
| L.A. 22 or 21: Plant Mat.†... | 2 | 2 |
| L.A. 31: Construction........ | 1 | 1.5 |
| Arch. 14: Freehand Draw. IV.. | 0.5 | 0.5 |
| Arch. 21: Water Color I...... | ¾ | .. |
| Arch. 22: Water Color II..... | .. | ¾ |
| Totals.................... | 8.25 | 8.75 |
| Professional Units.......... | 17 | |
| Geol. 3: Gen'l Principles...... | 1.5 | 1.5 |
| English Electives............ | 1 | 1 |
| P.E. 3: Physical Education or M.T. 3: Military Training | 0.5 | 0.5 |
| Totals.................... | 3 | 2 |
| Non-Professional Units...... | 5 | |
| Total Third-Year Units..... | 22 | |

## FOURTH YEAR—UPPER JUNIOR

| Subject and Number of Course | Units 1st Term | 2d Term |
|---|---|---|
| L.A. 3: Design, Class B....... | 6 | 6 |
| L.A. 24: Elementary Planting Design............. | 2 | 2 |
| L.A. 32: Construction........ | 1.5 | 1.5 |
| Arch. 15: Freehand Draw. V... | 0.5 | 0.5 |
| Arch. 23: Water Color........ | 0.5 | 0.5 |
| Totals.................... | 10.5 | 10.5 |
| Professional Units.......... | 21 | |
| P.E. 4: Physical Education or M.T. 4: Military Training... | 0.5 | 0.5 |
| Totals.................... | 0.5 | 0.5 |
| Non-Professional Units...... | 1 | |
| Total, Fourth-Year Units.... | 22 | |

## FIFTH YEAR—SENIOR

| Subject and Number of Course | Units 1st Term | 2d Term |
|---|---|---|
| L.A. 4: Design, Class A....... | 9 | 9 |
| L.A. 47: Prof. Practice....... | .. | 1 |
| Arch. 24: Water Color........ | 1 | .. |
| Arch. 25: Modelling......... | 1 | 1 |
| Arch. 45: Hist. Painting...... | .. | 1 |
| Arch. 46: Hist. Sculpture..... | 1 | .. |
| Totals.................... | 12 | 12 |
| Total, Fifth-Year Units...... | 24 | |

\* For adequate reasons other modern language courses may be substituted.
‡ Not required if student elects Arch. 42, 43 or 44.
† Subject given in alternate years.
NOTE: For description of subjects, see pages 49 to 66.

The first graduate of the landscape architecture program was a 39-year-old woman named Edith Crosby Stuart neé Brown. She received her B.L.A. in 1930, four years before women were graduating from Penn with degrees in architecture.

"Women had been admitted to the Towne Science program as early as the 1870s and were admitted to the Department of Architecture for courses. But they were not allowed in the life drawing course, on the grounds that it would be distracting for the men and embarrassing for the women. In a contradiction worthy of the military, life drawing was a requirement to receive the architecture degree; thus, women could graduate from Penn as architects only if they were willing to commute to Columbia where no such restriction existed. None did so.

The first woman would not receive an architecture degree until the late 1930s, when the dramatic reduction of the student body caused by the Depression forced Penn to change."

-"The Book of the School", Strong and Thomas

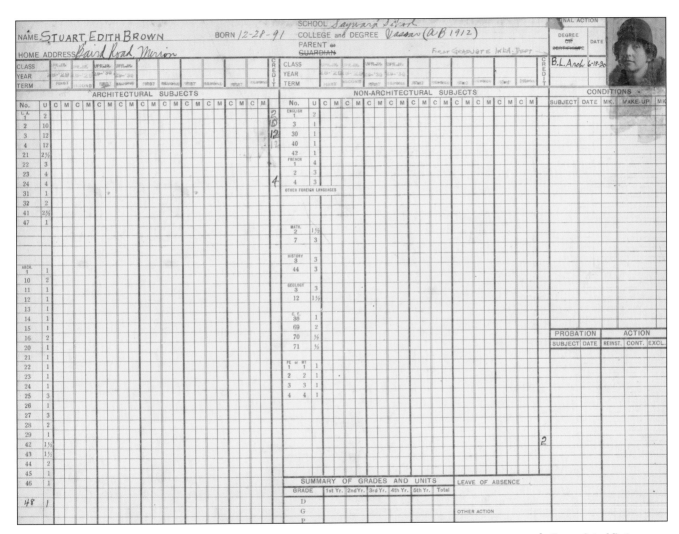

**Transcript of first graduate**

Stuart was the first to finish the five year B.L.A. program

1930

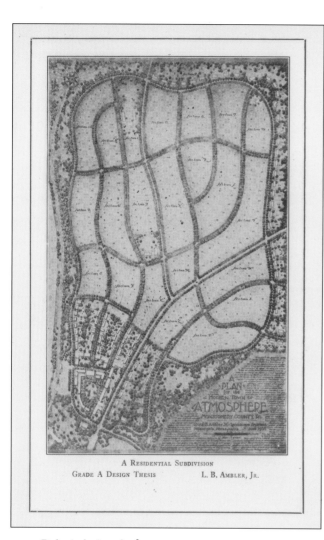

A RESIDENTIAL SUBDIVISION
GRADE A DESIGN THESIS          L. B. AMBLER, JR.

A COUNTRY ESTATE
GRADE A DESIGN, 1st MENTION, L. B. AMBLER
INTER-SCHOOL PROBLEM

**Early student work**

A residential subdivision
and an estate by
L.B. Ambler, Jr.

1931

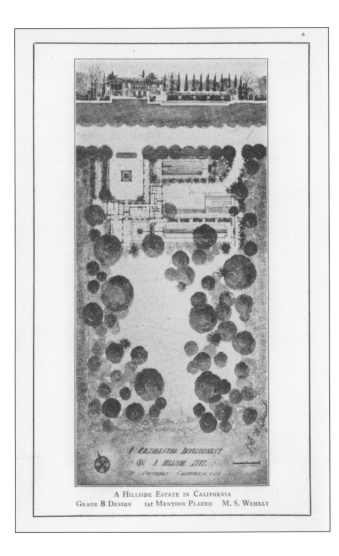

A HILLSIDE ESTATE IN CALIFORNIA
GRADE B DESIGN    1ST MENTION PLACED    M. S. WEHRLY

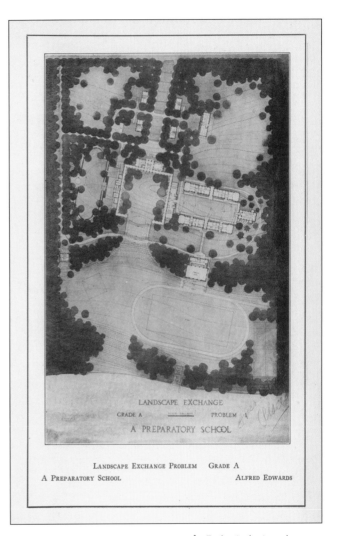

LANDSCAPE EXCHANGE PROBLEM    GRADE A
A PREPARATORY SCHOOL    ALFRED EDWARDS

**Early student work**

An estate by M.S. Wehrly
and a preparatory school
by Alfred Edwards

1933

In 1939, Wheelwright introduced a one-year graduate program in landscape architecture, expanding upon the existing five-year undergraduate program. At a time of reduced student enrollment and uncertain futures, this was a bold move. A few months later, the Selective Service Act was passed, the first peacetime draft in United States history, and a year after that the United States entered World War II. The war, in addition to the Depression, put tremendous strain on the school. Student enrollment continued to decline, and Wheelwright was left to run the program alone, until he also registered for the draft in 1942. Without a chair and with just four students remaining, the program was suspended.

# 1934-1943

One-year Master of
Landscape Architecture
(M.L.A.) degree offered

Landscape architecture
program suspended

| | |
|---|---|
| **Dust Bowl begins** | 1934 |
| **Everglades National Park established** | |
| Wright's Citizens' Petition for Broadacre City | |
| **Dust Bowl mass migrations begin** | 1935 |
| **FBI established** | |
| **Social Security established** | |
| Wright's Fallingwater | |
| Steele's Naumkeag | |
| **First artificial heart invented** | 1936 |
| LIFE magazine, first issue | |
| Savage's Hoover Dam, world's tallest dam (until 1959) | |
| **Hindenberg disaster** | 1937 |
| **Jet engine invented** | |
| Strauss, Morrow and Ellis' Golden Gate Bridge, world's longest suspension bridge (until 1964) | |
| Eckbo, Rose & Kiley's "Design Manifesto" | 1938 |
| Well's "War of the World's" broadcast | |
| Mumford's "The Culture of Cities" | |
| **World War II begins** | 1939 |
| World's Fair in NYC | |
| Best Picture "Gone with the Wind" | |
| **Selective Service Act, first peacetime draft in US history** | 1940 |
| **US enters World War II** | 1941 |
| **Manahattan Project begins** | |
| Asplund's Woodland Cemetery | |
| **Fermi splits the atom** | 1942 |
| **First computer invented** | |
| **Detroit race riots** | 1943 |
| Best Picture "Casablanca" | |

Hayden Hall, home of
School of Fine Arts

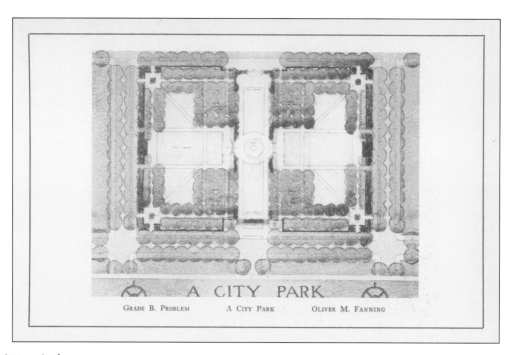

A CITY PARK

GRADE B. PROBLEM          A CITY PARK          OLIVER M. FANNING

**Early student work**

A city park by
Oliver M. Fanning

1934

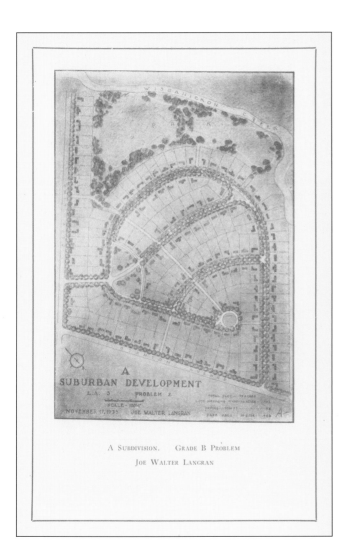

A SUBDIVISION.  GRADE B PROBLEM

JOE WALTER LANGRAN

GRADE A PROBLEM.  LOW RENT HOUSING PROJET

JOE WALTER LANGRAN

**Early student work**

A suburban housing
develoment and a low-rent
housing project by Joe
Walter Langran

# 1935, 1937

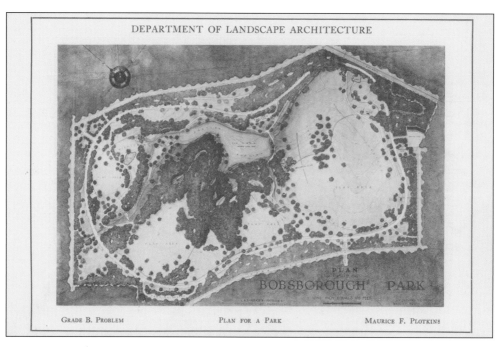

DEPARTMENT OF LANDSCAPE ARCHITECTURE

PLAN
BOBSBOROUGH PARK

GRADE B. PROBLEM          PLAN FOR A PARK          MAURICE F. PLOTKINS

**Early student work**

A plan for a park
by Maurice F. Plotkins

In 1939, Wheelwright introduced a one-year M.L.A degree. Course requirements were similar to that of the undergraduate program, but were of an abbreviated scope and timeframe. Master's students were also required to submit a thesis before graduating.

The course in Landscape Architecture seeks, in so far as possible, within the limitations of time, to present a broad and liberal culture as a background for professional activities. The Department of Landscape Architecture of the University of Pennsylvania is a member of the Association of Professional Schools of Landscape Architecture and the course is organized to prepare students for the practice of Landscape Architecture in accord with the standards and principles of the American Society of Landscape Architects.

## THE GRADUATE COURSE IN LANDSCAPE ARCHITECTURE

Advanced instruction in Landscape Architecture is offered in a graduate course which leads to the degree of Master of Landscape Architecture. Candidates for this degree must complete a minimum of forty-eight semester credits of work over and above the requirements for a bachelor's degree.

Opportunity is given in this course for research study in landscape design and planting design comparable to that which is done by students who receive travelling scholarships in Europe.

The region of Philadelphia offers unusual opportunities to study executed design adapted to American life, both of an historical and contemporary character, not only in the immediate neighborhood, but in as easily accessible parts as the territory between New England and Virginia. An extraordinary advantage lies in the fact that no part of the United States supports such a wide range of plant materials. A major emphasis in research will be permitted according to the particular interest or need of the individual.

Required work in City and Regional Planning is such as to familiarize the student with the relationship of Public Planning projects of various types. A thesis will be required to qualify for the Master's degree.

## GRADUATE COURSE IN LANDSCAPE ARCHITECTURE

| Subject and its Title | Subject Number | Semester Credits | | Total Hours Allotted to Subject Per Week | |
|---|---|---|---|---|---|
| | | 1st Term | 2nd Term | 1st Term | 2nd Term |
| Graduate Design | L.A. 5 | 16 | 16 | 32 | 32 |
| Principles of City and Regional Planning | L.A. 52 | 4 | — | 8 | — |
| Research in City and Regional Planning | L.A. 53 | — | 4 | — | 8 |
| Electives‡ | | 4 | 4 | 8 | 8 |
| Minimum Totals Required | | 24 | 24 | 48 | 48 |

‡ Electives shall be taken in subjects with the approval of the chairman of the Department of Landscape Architecture, and at least 4 s.c. in Freehand Drawing.

NOTE.—A description of the Professional Subjects in Landscape Architecture is shown on pages 96 to 98. The architectural subjects of the course appear on pages 83 to 88, those in Civil Engineering on page 89, and the academic subjects on pages 88 to 106.

From 1924 to 1941, 64 students (40 men, 24 women, aged 18 to 47) passed through the landscape architecture program. Three B.F.A.s and 23 B.L.A.s were awarded.

In 1942, the program was suspended after Wheelwright, program director, registered for the draft.

From 1942 onward, the landscape architecture program was suspended, although it was still authorized to award B.L.A. degrees. Frederick Peck, a graduate of the program, taught a limited number of courses in 1948 and again in 1951, but it was a new dean, G. Holmes Perkins, who truly revitalized the program. Perkins ideals were established at Harvard under Jean Jacques Haffner, and he sought to create a school balanced between architecture, landscape architecture and city planning. Perkins introduced a new Department of Land and City Planning in his very first year as dean, and the following year established a program in landscape architecture, offering a five-year B.L.A. degree. The year after that, the program expanded to offer a one-year M.L.A. Perkins brought swift and dramatic change to the school and his influence resonated for decades to come.

# 1944-1953

Two courses in
landscape architecture
by Peck, no formal
degree offered

Perkins becomes
dean of the school,
Department of Land
and City Planning
established

Program of landscape
architecture
established, five-year
B.L.A. offered

One-year M.L.A. offered

44

| | |
|---|---|
| Harry Truman, US Vice President, assumes presidency on FDR's death<br>G.I. Bill passes | 1944 |
| US drops nuclear bombs on Japan<br>World War II ends<br>United Nations established | 1945 |
| British New Towns Act<br>ENIAC or "Giant Brain", world's first electronic computer, built at Penn<br>Neutra's Kaufmann House | 1946 |
| UFO crash in Roswell, New Mexico<br>Corbusier's Unite d'Habitation<br>Levittown, NY, first planned community in US, receives first residents | 1947 |
| Harry Truman elected US President<br>First polaroid camera sold<br>Ghandi assassinated<br>Church's Donnell Garden<br>Pollock's "Composition No 1"<br>Leopold's "A Sand County Almanac" | 1948 |
| Berlin Blockade splits Germany into two separate German states<br>NATO established<br>Clarke's "Landscape into Art"<br>Geddes "Cities in Evolution", new edition | 1949 |
| US enters Korean War<br>McCarthyism begins<br>"I Love Lucy" show sparks<br>Golden Age of Television | 1950 |
| First commercial computer sold<br>Mies van der Rohe's Farnsworth House<br>J. B. Jackson founds "Landscape"<br>Salinger's "Catcher in the Rye"<br>Kerouac's "On the Road" | 1951 |
| Dwight Eisenhower elected US President<br>First British test of nuclear bomb on Montebello Islands, Australia<br>US New Town development begins in Reston, VA | 1952 |
| Korean War ends<br>First color television sold<br>Watson and Clark discover DNA<br>Shepheard's "Modern Gardens" | 1953 |

World War II battle training at Penn

45

**G. Holmes Perkins**

As part of his agreement to come to Penn, Perkins asked University President Harold Stassen for authority to establish new departments in landscape architecture and city planning. At the time, Perkins assumed that he would be rejected, but that was not the case.

"I said I wouldn't think of coming unless he agreed to this. I figured that was the end of that, but he said okay, right then and there."

-"The Book of the School", Strong and Thomas

1948

Initially, landscape architecture was taught under the Department of Land and City Planning, created by Perkins in 1951.

"Landscape architecture like its partners, architecture and city planning, is a social art... The closeness of their respective interests and their mutual dependence makes it obvious that each will gain by the development of healthy habits of working together."

-School of Fine Arts Bulletin 1951

## LANDSCAPE ARCHITECTURE

Landscape architecture like its partners, architecture and city planning, is a social art. Its practitioners offer those services whereby the earth's surface is moulded for human use and enjoyment. All three professions quite properly share common objectives and to a large degree similar ways of working. Yet each has its special techniques and areas of unique competence which are not shared by the others. The closeness of their respective interests and their mutual dependence makes it obvious that each will gain by the development of healthy habits of working together, by which method alone a higher standard of service can be given the community.

The primary objectives of the first year are to acquaint the student with the creative manner of working which is common to all of the arts of design, while at the same time providing him with the technical tools with which he must tackle increasingly complex problems in his later years. These habits of thought and of vision are not to be gained through the mere accumulation of factual knowledge nor by the imposition of dogma but can only be gained through the repeated personal experience of the student.

The inseparability of these experiences is fostered by the methods of attacking each problem. By personal field investigation, by visits to neighborhoods and communities, by study of the social and economic problems of the family and of the forms of social and political organization, and by first-hand contact with the city and rural landscape, the student prepares, under guidance, the programs which form the basis for his designs.

The central discipline in landscape architecture is found in the successive drafting room courses. Here are brought together as an indissoluble unity a concept of space, structure, and materials which grows out of the needs of man and his resources. An emphasis is placed upon the larger aspects of landscape architecture with particular reference to the myriad problems with which our cities are today faced by their rapid expansion and the ensuing need for redevelopment, by the growing recognition of man's leisure needs, and by a deepening consciousness of the necessity of conserving our dwindling natural resources. The landscape architect is a key figure in the creation of plans for new housing, city parks and playgrounds, parkways, new towns and state and national parks. In each he must be prepared by training and experience to work in harmony with architects and planners. By continuous collaboration in his school work and by constant contact with reality in each problem, the student is enabled to enter the profession better prepared to serve his client and community.

**Program description**

Outline of 5 year B.L.A. program under Perkins

1951

**Plan of Study: LANDSCAPE ARCHITECTURE**

| Year | Course | Subject | Hours 1st Term | 2nd Term |
|------|--------|---------|---------|----------|
| I | Design 100 | Design Fundamentals | 8 | 8 |
| | Math. 17a & b | Math. Analysis | 3 | 3 |
| | Eng. 102-103 | English Composition | 3 | 3 |
| | * | General Education | 5 | 5 |
| | P.E. 1 | Physical Education | 1 | 1 |
| II | Arch. 200 | Architecture and L.A. | 10 | 10 |
| | Eng. 130-140 | English Language & Lit. | 3 | 3 |
| | Arch. 230 | Matls. & Methods of Const. | 2 | 2 |
| | F.A. 140 | History of Art | 3 | 3 |
| | P.E. 2 | Physical Education | 1 | 1 |
| III | Arch. 300 | Arch., City Pl. & L.A. | 10 | 10 |
| | L.A. 331 | Landscape Construction | 3 | 3 |
| | L.A. 330 | Plant Materials | 3 | 3 |
| | F.A. 441, 442, 443, 444, 445 | Hist. of Arch., L.A. & C.P. | 3 | 3 |
| IV | L.A. 400 | Landscape Design | 10 | 10 |
| | L.A. 431 | Municipal & Site Engineering | 3 | — |
| | L.A. 432 | Landscape Construction | — | 3 |
| | * | General Education | 3 | 3 |
| | | Elective | 3 | 3 |
| V | L.A. 501 | Landscape Design | 12 | — |
| | L.A. 502 | Thesis | — | 15 |
| | * | General Education | 3 | 3 |
| | L.A. 531 | Prof. Practice & Specifications | 3 | — |

*General Education requirements: a minimum of 6 s. c. in each of the three fields of the humanities (philosophy, history, foreign languages and literature, music, American civilization), social sciences (economics, political science, sociology, social anthropology, economic geography, social psychology), and natural sciences (chemistry, physics, botany, zoology, earth sciences). Only courses of a general educational nature in these areas will be accepted.

**Course listing**

Early studios were a joint effort between city planning, architecture and landscape architecture

1952

From 1952-1954, landscape architecture was part of a new curriculum based on a shared program in which undergraduates in architecture, city planning and landscape architecture were taught together for the first three years, before splitting into their separate programs for the last two.

"The work of the first three years of the professional courses in architecture, city planning and landscape architecture is, except in rare cases, identical in content, reflecting the fact that all are parts of a common field."

-"The Book of the School", Strong and Thomas

This shared model did not last long. Perkins still had faith in the system he had created but other design schools, such as MIT and Harvard, had begun shifting attention away from undergraduate programs towards graduate education. In order for Penn to remain competitive, Perkins needed to establish graduate level training in landscape architecture.

In 1953, Perkins invited Ian McHarg, a former planning student of his from Harvard, to come from Scotland and build a new Department of Landscape Architecture.

**Ian McHarg**

McHarg served in the Parachute Regiment in World War II, before beginning his landscape architecture career

1954

In Ian McHarg, Perkins found an ideal chair for his new Department of Landscape Architecture. McHarg had studied planning under Perkins at Harvard and had received his M.L.A. and M.C.P. from there. McHarg worked for a time in Scotland, but was lured away by Perkins' offer to establish a new program at Penn. He taught from 1954 onwards, becoming the official chair of the department in 1957. In 1958, the School of Fine Arts became the Graduate School of Fine Arts, an indication of the changes Perkins was making in curriculum, faculty appointments, research opportunities and the addition of graduate level programs. Perkins also used his influence to build and maintain a rare book collection at the school, as well as ensuring that the Fine Arts Library collection was not subsumed when the larger Van Pelt Library was constructed. In 1959, the school hosted an international conference on urban design, which solidified its pre-eminence in the fields of city planning, urbanism and landscape architecture. Prestigious attendees ranged from Lewis Mumford to Jane Jacobs to Louis Kahn.

# 1954-1963

Department of
Landscape Architecture
established, McHarg
becomes chair

Conference on urban
design criticism

McHarg begins
offering 'Man and the
Environment' course

| | |
|---|---|
| School segregation declared illegal<br>US tests hydrogen bomb at Bikini Atoll<br>First nuclear submarine, USS Nautilus | 1954 |
| Rosa Parks refuses to give up her seat<br>US involvement in Vietnam made official<br>Salk develops Polio vaccine<br>Kiley's Miller Garden<br>Disneyland opens | 1955 |
| Interstate Highway Act passed<br>Fidel Castro lands in Cuba<br>Computer language FORTRAN invented<br>Noguchi's UNESCO garden<br>Utzon's Sydney Opera House | 1956 |
| Soviets launch Sputnik, first Earth<br>satellite, space race begins<br>71 cities worldwide over 1 million people<br>Stein's "Toward New Towns for America"<br>Eiseley's "The Immense Journey" | 1957 |
| USS Nautilus first vessel to<br>pass under the North Pole<br>Mies van der Rohe's Seagram Building | 1958 |
| Castro's Cuban Revolution ends<br>Alaska and Hawaii become last US states<br>NASA founded<br>Wright's Guggenheim Museum<br>Eckbo's ALCOA Forecast Garden | 1959 |
| John F. Kennedy elected US President<br>Greensboro lunch counter sit-ins begin<br>World population, 3 million<br>Osmundson & Staley's Kaiser Roof Garden<br>Corbusier's Sainte Marie de La Tourette | 1960 |
| US breaks diplomatic relations with Cuba<br>Shepard, first American in space<br>Archigram founded<br>Jacobs "The Death and Life of<br>Great American Cities" | 1961 |
| Cuban missile crisis<br>Construction begins on Berlin Wall<br>Glenn, first American to orbit the Earth<br>Warhol's Marilyn portraits<br>Carson's "Silent Spring"<br>Gans' "The Urban Villagers" | 1962 |
| Dr. Martin Luther King Jr.'s<br>"I have a dream" speech<br>US President Kennedy assassinated<br>Freidan's "The Feminine Mystique" | 1963 |

Fine Arts Library,
interior

Once McHarg accepted Perkins' offer to head the new Department of Landscape Architecture, he immediately focused on the department's most pressing issue.

"The question was, if we had a graduate program, how would we compete with Harvard?

Harvard was admitting B.L.A.s exclusively, and we had to compete with them. And that's when I struck upon the stratagem of admitting architects and training them in landscape architecture. If we set up a program admitting only people with architecture degrees, we would solve the problem of inferiority of the landscape architect vis-a-vis the architect, since the people studying landscape architecture would already be skilled designers."

-Ian McHarg "The Book of the School", Strong and Thomas

Tudor
Wing

recruitment · preparing for attack ... [illegible]
continuing to attract foreign arch...
degree/graduate recruit undergrad
Cornell abandoned undergrade programme - ... grad prog.
remainder State colleges ...

recruitment.    foreign architects.    30
              beginning amer. archs.    2        grads.
              amer.  B.A. B.S.    4-6
              undergrads  least.

Cornell abandoned u'grad: purely grad prog.
only indep. Univ. with u'grad programme.
Harvard  6 yr.  for Master Degree.
— 4 BA — 1/2 MLA.

— Penn proposed   4 BA — 6 BLA — 7 MLA.
   Harvard        4 BA⁴ MLA 5.
                  4 BA other — 6.

only competition among grad schools
  is between Penn & Harvard.

                Penn        Harv.
now             BLA  MLA              Lift.
purely grad prog.  1 yr min.   1 yr. min.
BA/BS.    3½ yrs + sum.   2 yrs. no summer.
B Arch.   2 yrs. probably 1½ 2 yrs
prop.  BA  4              4
       BLA  6
       MLA  7            5th 6 other.
       out of competition with Harvard

Wareman

Restaurant placemat

McHarg's musings on
competing with Harvard

1954

## Landscape Architecture

### THE PROFESSION OF LANDSCAPE ARCHITECTURE

When the creation of shelter includes an appreciation of the quality of human experience, building becomes architecture; when the disposition of plant materials, inert materials, and water in the landscape includes an appreciation of the quality of open space, horticulture becomes landscape architecture. It is this concern with the quality of the environment created rather than simply the functions of open space, the characteristics of plant and inert materials, or the mechanics of modifying the ground forms, which must distinguish the practice of landscape architecture.

Such a concern has motivated design in the landscape historically and each epoch has contributed disciplines and techniques valid for the solution of contemporary problems. The ancient Egyptians demonstrated the fundamental functions of outdoor space—the provision of food and timber, shade and shelter, privacy and protection; the Moslem culture added the technique of exploitation and control of climate and micro-climate; the Renaissance contributed a virtuosity of technique; the eighteenth century English landscape tradition illuminates the importance of the biotic balance of nature as the prime determinant in design of the larger landscape while from China and Japan can be seen a symbolistic

**Program description**

Perkins maintained influence over the department even after McHarg's arrival

## 1957

McHarg taught for a few years at Penn before becoming chair, during which time he was exposed to Perkins' ideals regarding landscape architecture. In 1957, the department description and requirements were still defined by Perkins.

"When the creation of shelter includes an appreciation of the quality of human experience, building becomes architecture; when the disposition of plant materials, inert materials, and water in the landscape includes the appreciation of the quality of open space, horticulture becomes landscape architecture. It is this concern with the quality of the environment created rather than simply the functions of open space, the characteristics of plant and inert materials, or the mechanics of modifying the ground forms, which must distinguish the practice of landscape architecture."

-School of Fine Arts Bulletin 1957

By 1958, with McHarg now firmly established as chair, the department began to reflect his personal values and the direction he wanted to take landscape architecture education, as well as the profession.

"One of the most conspicuous failures of 20th century western society has been the environment created. Squalor and anarchy are more accurate descriptions than are efficiency and delight. This should cause no surprise when we consider that prevailing values esteem ephemeral consumer products over landscape and townscape. Indeed the new yet obsolescent automobile or refrigerator are more highly prized than the enduring social and physical environment. Despoiliation of landscape and the acccretion of ugliness are inevitable consequences of such prevailing values."

-School of Fine Arts Bulletin 1958

---

SCHOOL OF FINE ARTS

## LANDSCAPE ARCHITECTURE

One of the most conspicuous failures of 20th century western society has been the environment created. Squalor and anarchy are more accurately descriptive than are efficiency and delight. This should cause no surprise when we consider that prevailing values esteem the ephemeral consumer product over landscape and townscape. Indeed the new yet obsolescent automobile or refrigerator are much more highly prized than the enduring social and physical environment. Despoliation of landscape, the accretion of ugliness as cities are inevitable consequences of such prevailing values.

In the general failure to create an efficient and delightful setting for life, no .sector exhibits a greater popular indifference or ignorance than does the attitude towards the role of open space. Yet, historically where a noble and ennobling environment has been created, be it in the classical cities, 12th century Moslem Iberia, Italy in the Renaissance, 16th century Japan, or 18th century England, the quality of open space as agora, forum, garden, plaza, or landscape, has been the triumph of physical design, frequently the most meaningful expression of the society and generally its most humane physical expression.

Heredity, the cultural heritage, and environment are the three determinants of society. Geneticists and empiricists alike affirm the overwhelming role of environment, indeed recent scientific research accords it an importance much beyond that previously accredited. A significant change in values must occur before society appreciates the impact which the physical setting does make negatively today and can contribute positively tomorrow. The landscape architect has a role in affirming the importance of open space in the physical environment, he has no less a task in learning to manipulate as an artist the elements which are his tools—space, light-and-shadow, sticks, stones and water, trees, flowers, grasses, and the changing seasons.

No part of the creative process leading to efficient, beautiful and ennobling townscapes and landscapes presents a greater challenge than does the design of open-space—landscape architecture. Here the promise of vital social contribution is unmatched. It is, however, necessary to formulate a body of principle which encompasses the functions of open space in society and, further to develop formal expressions which are meaningful, evocative, and valued, and which bring function and delight to society through its environment. This challenge directs the landscape architect at least as much to the problems of the city as to those of suburb and countryside.

Technique, disciplines, and materials can be taught; principle of formal expression must be sought. Answers will be found in many places but a graduate program is an inevitable center for such a search. The graduate curricula are dedicated to the search for a body of principle and a formal expression for design in open space by which the landscape architect can make

**Program description**

McHarg significantly shifted the department description and courses once he became chair

1958

When the school held a conference on urban design in 1959, whose participants were some of the most well-known critics and thinkers of the day, it demonstrated that the Graduate School of Fine Arts was becoming the pre-eminent institution for landscape architecture, architecture and planning.

From left to right, William L.C. Wheaton, Lewis Mumford, Ian McHarg, J.B. Jackson, David A. Crane, Louis I. Kahn, G. Holmes Perkins, Arthur Holden, member of dean Perkin's staff, Catherine Bauer Wurster, Leslie Cheek, Jr., Mary Barnes, Jane Jacobs, Kevin Lynch, Gordon Stephenson, Nanine Clay, and I.M. Pei.

**Urban design conference group photo**

1959

# G. Holmes Perkins

**G. Holmes Perkins
design review**

Perkins, second from left

# Reflection

"Amid recurring political and social crisis, our modest problem of educating a new generation of architects gets scant attention. Nor does this appear surprising or unjust. Yet, on second thought, will not the vision, the dedication and the skill of architects play perhaps the decisive role in the creation of tomorrow's world which will be dominated by the city? The quality of the urban environment will mold our lives and thoughts. Nor do I see any inherent conflict with nature for man himself and all his works are but a manifestation of nature. At present, however, man's skill in the creation of new systems that promote and maintain an ecologic balance are sadly rudimentary. The science of urban ecology is in a most primitive state, and our understanding of social behavior only slightly more advanced. Under such circumstances it is hardly surprising that our architectural visions have been so limited, that we have to depend so heavily on intuition, that we have failed to reflect in our design the potential richness of modern social life and have relied too much upon norms and averages for guidance rather than upon an understanding of the individual whose ambitions and activities are legion. We have been so blinded by our own technical virtuosity that we have dared to challenge nature's laws rather than recognizing them as the best of guides."

-"Architectural Education," from an address to the Royal Academy of Architects

By the end of the 1950s, the School was becoming a victim of its own success, straining at the seams of its home at the time, Hayden Hall. A new fine arts building was proposed, and Louis Kahn, a professor in the Department of Architecture, was selected by Perkins. School politics influenced the decision, however, and Kahn was soon rejected. The ensuing design and construction process of what would ultimately become known as Meyerson Hall became fraught with student protests, often spurred on by professors and even McHarg himself. Simultaneous with the building construction was the development of a new program known as regional planning, taught under the auspices of both the Departments of Landscape Architecture and City Planning. To showcase the new program and direction, McHarg changed the department's title to Landscape Architecture and Regional Planning. Soon thereafter, McHarg released "Design with Nature", which definitively demonstrated his commitment to ecology as the basis of design, an ideal which began to permeate the whole of the department.

# 1964-1973

Two-year Master of
Regional Planning
(M.R.P.) degree offered

Sir Peter Shepheard
becomes dean of
the school

Center for Ecological
Research in Planning
and Design established

| | |
|---|---|
| Lyndon B. Johnson elected US President<br>Race riots across major US cities<br>Civil Rights Act, segregation made illegal<br>The Beatles appear on Ed Sullivan Show,<br>British invasion begins | 1964 |
| US escalates involvement in Vietnam<br>Malcolm X assassinated<br>Watts Riots in Los Angeles | 1965 |
| Hippie movement begins<br>Superstudio founded<br>Halprin's Lovejoy Plaza<br>WMRT begins Baltimore Inner Harbor | 1966 |
| Race riots across major US cities<br>Summer of Love<br>Safdie's Habitat<br>Fuller's Geodesic Dome<br>Halprin's Sea Ranch | 1967 |
| Richard Nixon elected US President<br>Dr. Martin Luther King Jr. and<br>Robert F. Kennedy assassinated<br>Fuller's "Operating Manual for<br>Spaceship Earth"<br>Ehrlich's "The Population Bomb" | 1968 |
| Armstrong walks on the moon<br>Woodstock music festival<br>Vietnam War demonstrations<br>McHarg's "Design with Nature"<br>Halprin's "RSVP Cycles" | 1969 |
| EPA established<br>Kent State Massacre<br>First Earth Day<br>Smithson's Spiral Jetty<br>Burle Marx's Copacabana | 1970 |
| US decreases voting age to 18 years<br>US bombs Cambodia and North Vietnam<br>Haag's Gas Works Park<br>Edward D. Stone Jr and Associate's<br>PepsiCo Headquarters | 1971 |
| Watergate scandal<br>Pruitt Igoe homes detonated<br>DDT is banned | 1972 |
| Roe v. Wade ruling legalizes abortion<br>US withdraws from Vietnam<br>First oil embargo leads to market crash<br>WMRT's Pardisan, initial plan | 1973 |

Fine Arts Building,
now Meyerson Hall

When it became apparent that Hayden Hall was no longer large enough for the school, students assumed that Kahn, their famed professor of architecture, would receive the commission to design the new building. The University rejected Kahn, however, because of issues over Kahn's recently built Richards Medical Laboratories and instead selected Overseer and Trustee Sydney Martin's firm of Martin, Stewart, Noble and Class.

The design, as well as the location of the building, immediately inflamed the student body and protests continued for several years. While most of the protests focused on the Save our Open Space campaign, with students even chaining themselves to trees that were to be removed, the consensus for the resentment lay in the rejection of Kahn as architect.

Kahn swore that he would never set foot in the building, choosing instead to run his studios from the adjacent Furness building (now the Fisher Fine Arts Library), although he did occasionally come over for happy hour.

"My first year, I had all my landscape courses in Hayden Hall, in a semi-submerged room with large windows, the sills of which were level with the grass outside. One evening, at midnight or so, McHarg came to check on us, climbing through the window wearing a full tuxedo." -Dennis McGlade, M.L.A. '69

**Fine Arts Building protest**

Students protested during the entirety of the design and construction process

1963

In 1963, Ian McHarg joined forces with fellow professors David Wallace, Bill Roberts and Tom Todd to form Wallace, McHarg, Roberts and Todd (WMRT). All four taught within the department, and at times it was difficult to differentiate between the firm and the school.

**Plan for the Valleys**

Rendered view by WMRT

"In a sense WMRT and the Landscape Architecture Department were largely indivisible. McHarg, Roberts, Narendra Juneja and others moved between the classroom and the office, using the University as a platform to formulate and test ideas then applied in the firm's professional projects and ultimately offered as studios."

-"The Book of the School", Strong and Thomas

The year of its founding, WMRT released the Plan for the Valleys, a seminal strategy for sustainable growth. The plan was commissioned by the Greenspring & Worthington Valley communities, who sought to protect the historic character and natural amenity of the area by planning for future development.

In 1980, McHarg left the firm, and it became WRT. It has since grown to over 100 people, with offices in Philadelphia, San Francisco and Miami, continuing its same values of ecological design, research and planning.

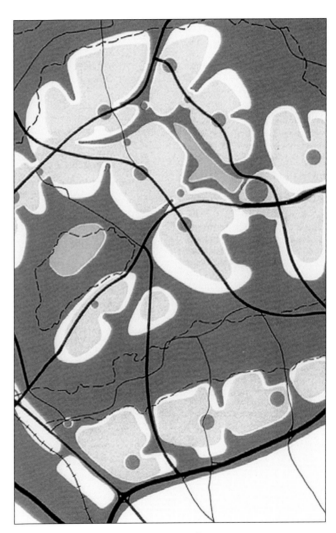

**Early work of WMRT**

Plan for the Valleys was one of WMRT's early projects, incorporating regional analysis with design thinking

1963

**Program announcement**

Description and requirements for M.R.P. degree

In 1965, McHarg started the regional planning program and renamed the department Landscape Architecture and Regional Planning. Created to explore larger scale planning projects that he felt could not be addressed within traditional city planning, the program was based on the tenets of ecology and the sciences, and was shared jointly with the Department of City Planning.

"The curriculum in Regional Planning offered in the Graduate School of Fine Arts consists of two 'streams' with a common core of planning courses. One stream is based upon preparation in the natural sciences in which the student enrolls through the Department of Landscape Architecture; the other stream is based upon preparation in the social sciences in which the student enrolls through the Department of City Planning. Both streams lead to the Master of Regional Planning degree at the end of two years of full-time study." -Graduate School of Fine Arts Bulletin 1965

McHarg also brought on several new professors in the mid 1960's, including Sir Peter Shepheard, who ultimately taught at Penn for over three decades, becoming dean of the school for five years during the mid 1970's, and Narendra Juneja, a former student of the program.

Juneja was a significant force within the school and the profession through his work at WMRT, before his untimely death in 1981 of a heart attack.

"Without Narendra, Ian could not have accomplished all that he did. There would be no "Design with Nature" as we know it. McHarg had the vision and did the writing, but Narendra orchestrated the whole." -Anne Whiston Spirn, M.L.A. '74

**Narendra Juneja**

Sketch by
Sir Peter Shepheard

1965

In their first years at Penn, Juneja and Shepheard developed in-depth analyses of their countries of origin. Both were talented artists and their drawings are impressive not only in their depth of information, but also in the beauty of their craftsmanship.

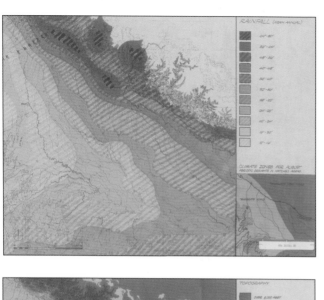

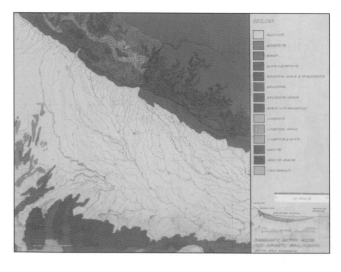

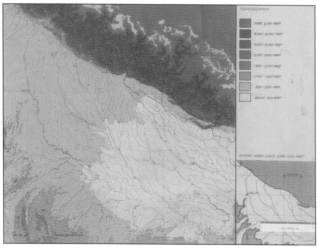

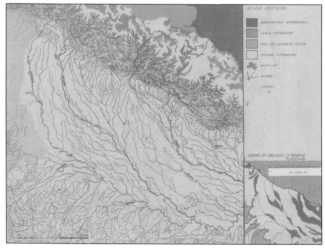

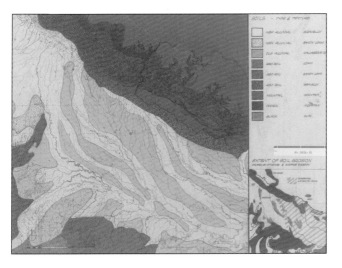
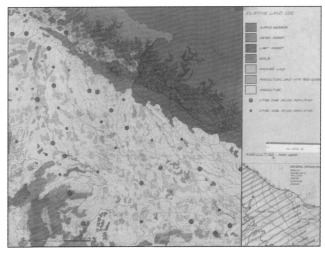
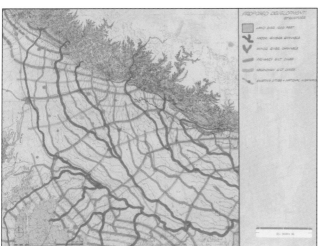
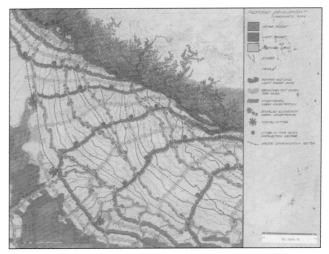

**Juneja's analysis of the
Upper Gangetic Plain
of India**

Mapping spanned from
geology to hydrology to
land form

1965

TOPOGRAPHY

PLANT COMMUNITIES

74

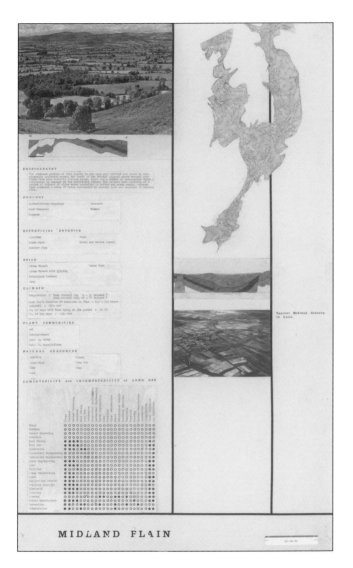

MIDLAND PLAIN

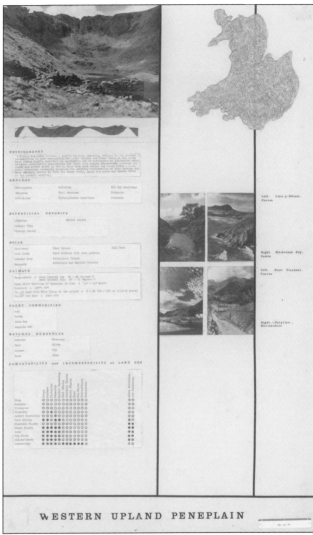

WESTERN UPLAND PENEPLAIN

**Shepheard's analysis of Great Britain**

Mapping included the entire continent

1965

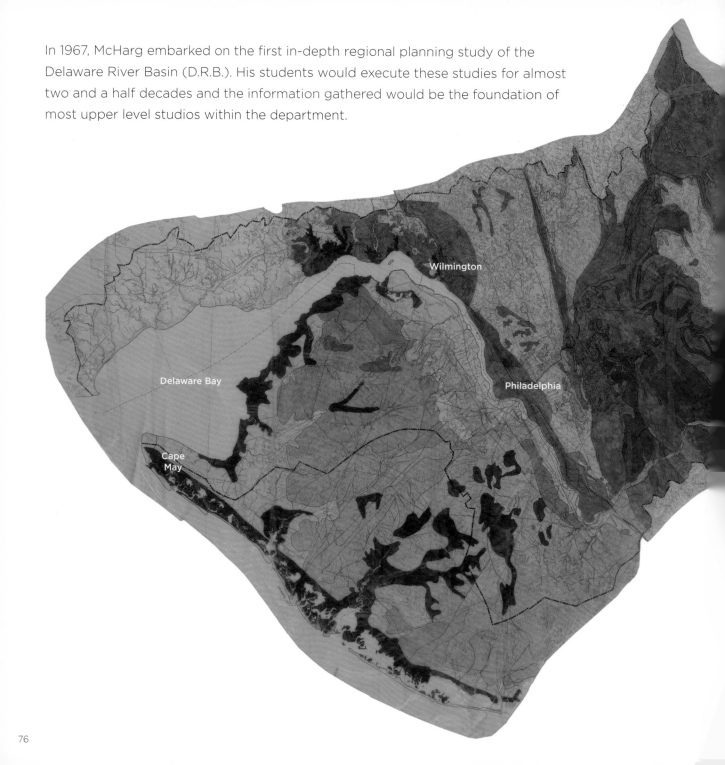

In 1967, McHarg embarked on the first in-depth regional planning study of the Delaware River Basin (D.R.B.). His students would execute these studies for almost two and a half decades and the information gathered would be the foundation of most upper level studios within the department.

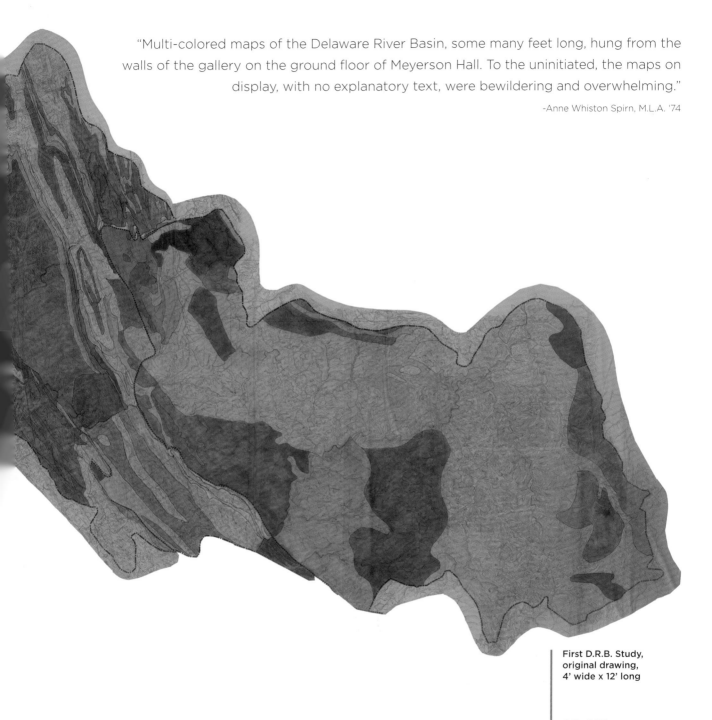

"Multi-colored maps of the Delaware River Basin, some many feet long, hung from the walls of the gallery on the ground floor of Meyerson Hall. To the uninitiated, the maps on display, with no explanatory text, were bewildering and overwhelming."

-Anne Whiston Spirn, M.L.A. '74

**First D.R.B. Study, original drawing, 4' wide x 12' long**

1967

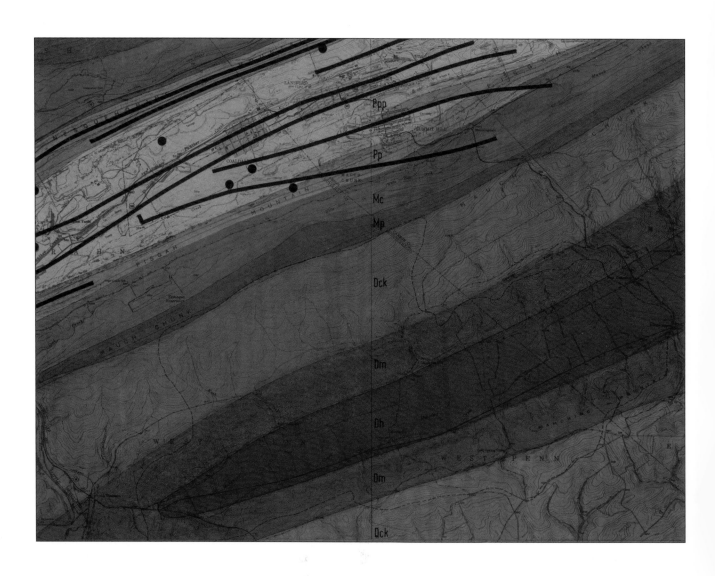

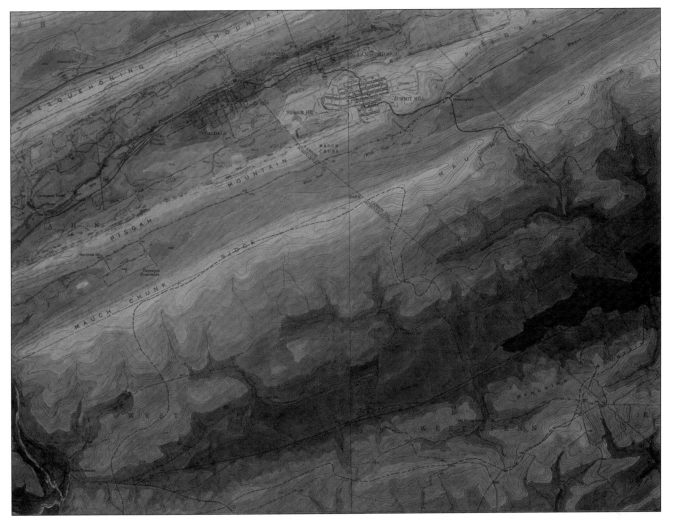

**Delaware River Basin II**

Analysis of geology and
elevation for second
iteration of D.R.B.

1968

"I remember McHarg once told me that he should be able to blindfold me, put me in a helicopter and randomly drop me off in one of the Delaware Valley regions we were studying. He said I should be able to identify where I was by interpreting the geology, topography, vegetation, wildlife and architecture.

That was how he introduced me to the concept of regionalism and it has stuck with me ever since."

-Terry Krinsky, M.L.A. '70

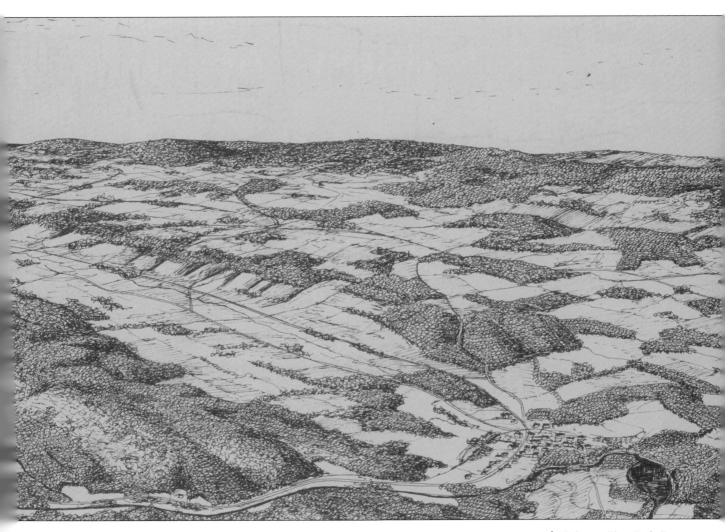

**Delaware River Basin II**

Illustration of the Delaware
River Basin

1968

In 1969, McHarg's seminal volume, "Design with Nature", was published. To date, it has sold almost 200,000 copies.

"Design With Nature" not only captured the burgeoning environmental zeitgeist of the 1970's, it also provided a practical method for the reconciliation of modernity and natural systems. Like his mentor, Lewis Mumford, McHarg held an arcadian image of culture and believed in the power of rational, or regional, planning to bring it about. Despite the limitations of the method and contradictions in the philosophy, McHarg's grand narrative of stewardship remains landscape architecture's *raison d'etre*.

"If one can view the biosphere as a single superorganism, then the Naturalist considers that man is an enzyme capable of its regulation, and conscious of it. He is of the system and entirely dependent upon it but has the responsibility for management, derived from apperception. This is his role—steward of the biosphere and its consciousness." -Ian McHarg, "Design with Nature"

"Ecology is to landscape architecture what gravity is to architecture."

-Rob Fisher, M.L.A. '70

**McHarg interview with Mike Douglas**

After the publication, McHarg was in demand from a variety of programs

1969

**Earth Week press conference**

McHarg and students in Meyerson Hall

The following year, "motivated by national press coverage of a speech that U.S. Senator Gaylord Nelson gave in the fall of 1969 in Seattle—in which he called for a national 'environmental teach-in', a group of University of Pennsylvania landscape architecture and regional planning students decided to organize not just an Earth Day, but an entire Earth Week of activities."

-"History of Earth Week", www.earthweek1970.org

Earth Week was a massive success, drawing tens of thousands of people each day to events from Independence Mall to Fairmount Park to the University itself.

U.S. Senator Edmund Muskie was the keynote speaker. Other attendees included Ian McHarg; presidential candidate Ralph Nader; Nobel prize-winning Harvard biochemist, George Wald; U.S. Senate Minority Leader, Hugh Scott; poet, Allen Ginsberg and the entire cast of "Hair".

Young girl at Earth Week celebration in Independence Mall

1970

**Sir Peter Shepheard**

In 1971, at the request of University President Martin Meyerson, Sir Peter Shepheard became dean of the school. This selection spoke both to the growing importance of the landscape architecture department, as well as Shepheard's abilities and rapport with students and faculty.

During Shepheard's eight-year tenure as dean, he developed a lecture series on landscape design called "Elements" that he continued for another two decades, he started an interdisciplinary undergraduate degree program in the design of the environment and he oversaw the development of a campus landscape plan that shaped Penn for years to come.

Shepheard was a great educator as well as a prolific artist. He used drawing as a way of seeing and of teaching. "Drawing a bird's wing—first the bones then the feathers—revealed the shape and structure that enable flight and demonstrated how drawing is not merely a form of expression, but also a form of inquiry."

-"Peter Shepheard", Annabel Downs

"Peter draws all the time, the way other people breathe." -Laurie Olin

**Drawing of a crow,
Sir Peter Shepheard**

1971

Within the school, McHarg and Shepheard created an atmosphere of cohesion and congeniality. Everyone worked hard, but they also played hard.

"As dean, Shepheard will be remembered best for two important contributions to the School and the University—the Design of the Environment program and the new campus landscape plan—as well as for the creation of Happy Hour."

-"The Book of the School", Strong and Thomas

McHarg's birthday party and "layer" cake

"Toward the end of a party at Ian's farm, Laurie began to dance with Victoria. Carol was in the house at the time so Ian grabbed the nearest small farm animal, a goat, held it to his chest and danced away!"

-Timothy Baird, M.L.A. '80

Sketches of Macintosh, McHarg and Muhlenberg by Laurie Olin

1971

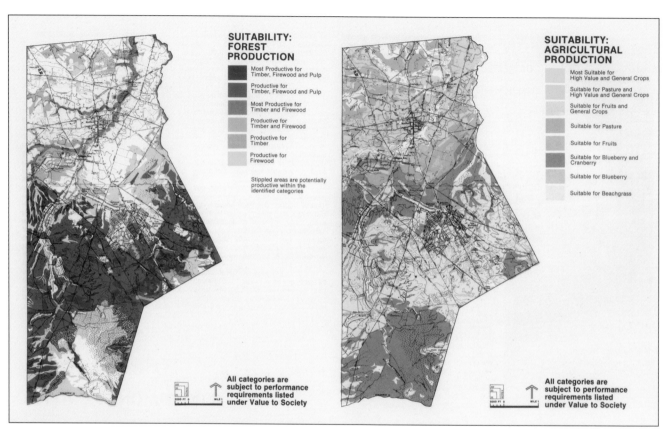

**SUITABILITY: FOREST PRODUCTION**

- Most Productive for Timber, Firewood and Pulp
- Productive for Timber, Firewood and Pulp
- Most Productive for Timber and Firewood
- Productive for Timber and Firewood
- Productive for Timber
- Productive for Firewood

Stippled areas are potentially productive within the identified categories

All categories are subject to performance requirements listed under Value to Society

**SUITABILITY: AGRICULTURAL PRODUCTION**

- Most Suitable for High Value and General Crops
- Suitable for Pasture and High Value and General Crops
- Suitable for Fruits and General Crops
- Suitable for Pasture
- Suitable for Fruits
- Suitable for Blueberry and Cranberry
- Suitable for Blueberry
- Suitable for Beachgrass

All categories are subject to performance requirements listed under Value to Society

**Medford Study, analysis maps**

Mapping defined areas for growth and protection

90

In 1972, in response to the growing ecological design movement, McHarg established the Center for Ecological Research in Planning and Design under the auspices of the school. The center undertook a multitude of design and research projects, beginning with the Medford study, a landmark model that enabled the town to successfully control its growth and maintain its surrounding environment. The plan is still utilized as a basis of planning decisions today.

"(The people of Medford) observed that traditional planning and zoning had been totally incapable of averting destruction in their neighboring communities. They hoped for a better future for Medford and suggested an ecological study be undertaken, oriented not to the preparation of a plan, but to the formulation of ordinances." -Medford Study, 1974

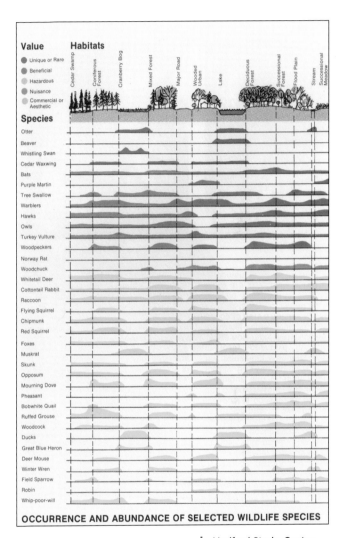

OCCURRENCE AND ABUNDANCE OF SELECTED WILDLIFE SPECIES

Medford Study, Center for Ecological Research in Planning and Design

1974

# Ian McHarg

# Reflection

Say—matter, of this is the universe, the world and life made.
Sun—shine that we may live.
Earth—home.
Oceans—ancient home.
Rain, rivers and streams—replenish from the oceans,
We erstwhile sea creatures removed from the sea by
only the length of a cell.
Atmosphere—protect and sustain us.
Plants—live, breathe and grow that we may eat,
breathe and live.
Decomposers—reconstitute the wastes of life and
the substance of death that life may endure.

-"An Ecological Prayer"

# Frederick 'Fritz' Steiner, M.R.P. '77 on Ian McHarg

Ian McHarg always viewed himself as both a landscape architect and a planner. This dual identity was rooted in his academic background at Harvard. He came from Scotland to Cambridge, Massachusetts to study landscape architecture. At Harvard, he found the modernism advanced by Walter Gropius and others in architecture and city planning more stimulating than what he perceived as a conservative emphasis on estate design for the wealthy in landscape architecture. To a large degree, this reflected a rift which had occurred between landscape architecture and city planning at Harvard several years earlier.

Harvard President Charles William Eliot founded the program in 1900 to honor his son (also Charles Eliot), who had been a pioneering landscape architect (and planner) and who had died in 1897 prematurely. The first Harvard teachers included Frederick Law Olmsted, Jr. and Arthur Shurtleff (later Shurcliff), both landscape architects and pioneers of the planning profession in the United States. Increasingly, the interests of the Harvard landscape architecture faculty were divided between site scale design and larger city planning concerns. This led to the establishment of Harvard's School of City Planning in 1929. Whereas city planning at Harvard focused on larger scale and social issues, landscape architecture retained a smaller scale orientation. McHarg earned degrees in both landscape architecture and city planning at Harvard.

He collaborated with three architecture students for their thesis, which involved the renovation of downtown Providence, Rhode Island.

Against this backdrop, in 1954, McHarg's former Harvard planning professor, G. Holmes Perkins, invited him to restart Penn's landscape architecture department. From the offset, McHarg had a joint appointment with city planning. As Penn's dean, Perkins sought to recreate the Graduate School of Design model developed by Harvard Dean Joseph Hudnut with departments of architecture, landscape architecture and city planning.

Like the younger Olmsted before him, McHarg was drawn to the broader societal challenges presented by planning. He also came to view an understanding of ecology as fundamental to the advancement of both design and planning. Beyond the academy, McHarg's practice, founded with city planner David Wallace, thrived. Conceived as an interdisciplinary firm, their other two partners, Tom Todd and Bill Roberts, had backgrounds in architecture, landscape architecture, and city planning. Eventually, McHarg created a parallel degree in regional planning at Penn and added it to the department's name, the Department of Landscape and Regional Planning.

This is the program I entered at Penn, and the combination of the two fields, both grounded in ecology, especially human ecology, has been a benefit to my career. I viewed my Penn regional planning education as larger scale landscape architecture. For a while, both landscape architecture and regional planning thrived together at Penn. However, after McHarg's retirement and with the rise of neoliberalism under the Ronald Reagan administration, planning floundered. Unlike his landscape architecture predecessors at Harvard, McHarg failed to institutionalize his planning vision at Penn.

McHarg's failure was due to at least three other factors. First, Penn already had a Department of City and Regional Planning. As a result, there was some perceived redundancy. Second, younger faculty wanted to focus more on urban design and less on ecology. Third, reflecting the influence of his mentors, Perkins and Lewis Mumford, McHarg used the name "regional planning." In reality, the program would be more accurately described as landscape or environmental or, as McHarg preferred, ecological planning. Had McHarg used one of these modifiers, then I believe its chances for survival would have been enhanced. At the very least, its stunning interdisciplinary innovation would be more widely known and appreciated.

Where does this leave us today? Once again, landscape architects, for the most part, have reinvented urbanism, this time calling it landscape urbanism and ecological urbanism and landscape ecological urbanism. Will it again spin away from landscape architecture as city planning did at Harvard in the 1920s? Or, disappear as ecologically based regional planning did at Penn in the 1990s? Or, might landscape architects again lead the urban agenda but sustain that leadership?

Meanwhile, the global environmental issues that McHarg challenged have not gone away. With climate change and urbanization, the plight of communities and regions has grown more alarming. Simultaneously, planning has moved increasingly from the physical world towards applied social science and public policy. Mainstream design has grown more dismissive of planning and its constraints. More and more, we increasingly need planners who understand design and designers who recognize what Charles Eames knew, "design depends largely on constraints." We also need planners and designers who are ecologically literate. We need to design and plan with nature.

From his beginnings as dean in 1971, Sir Peter Shepheard continued Perkins' vision for a unified school of landscape architecture, architecture and planning. In 1977, Shepheard coordinated one of his most significant contributions to the University in the form of a master plan of Penn's campus. In collaboration with Carol and Colin Franklin, Leslie and Rolf Sauer, Robert Hanna and Laurie Olin, and Narendra Juneja, the plan restored the campus landscape and saved it from decades of unchecked growth. McHarg did well under Shepheard's leadership, continuing to grow the Regional Planning Department to the point that it became, for a time, more popular than the Landscape Architecture Department. McHarg also introduced a wider scope of research at the behest of the National Institute of Mental Health, incorporating more social sciences, ethology, ethnography and anthropology.

# 1974-1983

Landscape
Development Plan for
campus created

Lee Copeland becomes
dean of the school

| | |
|---|---|
| Nixon resigns, Gerald Ford, US Vice President, assumes presidency<br>World population, 4 billion<br>Best Picture "The Godfather" | 1974 |
| Microsoft founded<br>Highest US unemployment since 1941<br>Best Picture "One Flew Over the Cuckoo's Nest" | 1975 |
| Jimmy Carter elected US President<br>Viking I & II land on Mars<br>Chairman Mao Tse-Tung dies<br>Halprin's Freeway Park<br>Best Picture "Rocky" | 1976 |
| First personal computer sold<br>Elvis Presley dies<br>US Department of Energy established<br>Best Picture "Annie Hall" | 1977 |
| Birth of first test tube baby<br>Amoco Cadiz oil spill<br>Shah of Iran imposes martial law | 1978 |
| Three Mile Island nuclear disaster<br>Iranian Revolution<br>Second oil embargo<br>Iranian hostage crisis begins<br>Schwartz's Bagel Garden | 1979 |
| Ronald Reagan elected US President<br>Mt. St. Helens erupts<br>John Lennon assassinated<br>Hargreaves' Harlequin Plaza<br>Noguchi's California Scenario | 1980 |
| First known AIDS death<br>O'Connor first female on Supreme Court<br>IBM introduces DOS launguage<br>Serra's "Tilted Arc"<br>Duany and Plater-Zyberk's Seaside<br>"Landscape Journal" founded | 1981 |
| Kahn's National Assembly of Bangladesh completed<br>Lin's Vietnam Veteran's Memorial | 1982 |
| First minivan sold<br>US Embassy in Beirut bombed<br>IBM computers now with hard drives<br>Best Picture "Terms of Endearment" | 1983 |

College Hall Green

With the arrival of Yehudi Cohen in 1971 and Dan Rose and Setha Low in 1974, the department entered a new era of social analysis. Social processes, personal interviews and mapping exercises began to be taught in core studios, and research into community life and social ideals added to the already rigourous scientific analysis that McHarg instituted throughout the department.

While McHarg's method did not readily engage social phenomena, he respected the importance of the research and used the data in concurrence with mapping exercises.

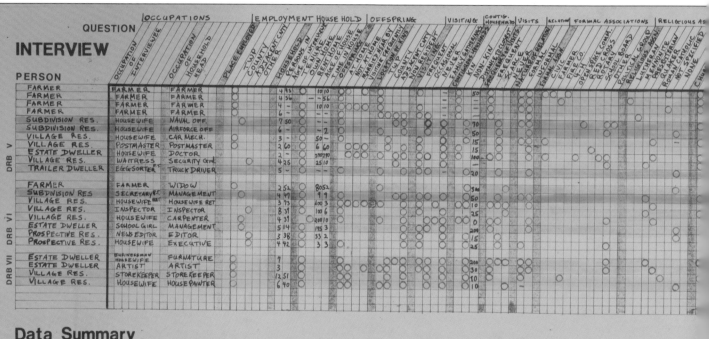

## Data Summary

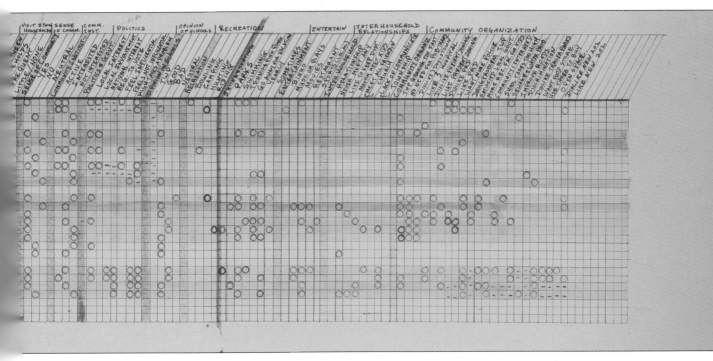

1974

**Andropogon founders
at Morris Arboretum;
Shoemaker Green**

The firm's first and most
recent commissions for
the University

In 1975, four students from the school, Carol Franklin, Colin Franklin, Leslie Sauer and Rolf Sauer, founded a landscape architecture firm based firmly in the ecological principles espoused by McHarg. They named their firm Andropogon, after a common field grass.

"Wherever the landscape has been disturbed, Andropogon is one of the first field grasses to colonize the ground, providing a cover for the gradual return of our native forests. The economy and elegance with which these grassy meadows heal the wounded landscape aptly describes Andropogon's goal in ecological planning and design, to weave together the landscape of man and nature for the benefit of both."

-Firm Philosophy, Andropogon

Today, Andropogon, led by Penn alumni José Almiñana and Yaki Miodovnik, continues to bring a rigorous ecological perspective to landscape architecture, enabling the practice to implement solutions and technologies that result in truly sustainable sites.

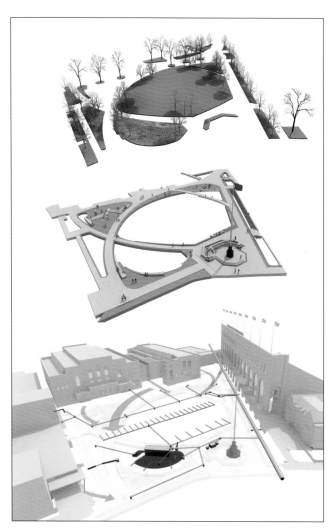

**Stormwater diagrams for Shoemaker Green**

**Bob Hanna and
Laurie Olin**

In 1976, Robert Hanna and Laurie Olin, both professors in the department, founded the landscape architecture and urban design studio of Hanna/Olin.

Hanna and Olin's design style influenced studios for decades at Penn and led to numerous award-winning projects within their firm, such as Bryant Park and Battery Park City in New York City, and the planning and design of Canary Wharf in London. In 1996, Hanna left the firm, which then became Olin Partnership and now is known simply as OLIN.

"OLIN is dedicated to affecting positive change through landscape architecture, urban design and planning. (We) are advocates for the artful creation and transformation of the public realm, and practice in a range of scales, including ecological and regional systems, urban districts, campuses, civic parks, plazas and intimate gardens." -Firm Philosophy, OLIN

**Bryant Park and Battery Park City, New York City**

These parks are two of Hanna/Olin's most iconic early projects

**College Hall Green
before renovation**

By the late 1970's, College Hall Green, the center of Penn's campus, was a maze of criss crossing dirt pathways and trampled mud patches. While the University had spent millions in the 1960's and 1970's on new buildings, it had neglected the landscape. Shepheard envisioned a "properly organized plan" that unified the campus, and solicited help from professors within the landscape architecture department, Carol and Colin Franklin, Leslie and Rolf Sauer (Andropogon), Robert Hanna and Laurie Olin (Hanna/Olin), and Narendra Juneja (WMRT), to create it.

"A plan is an instrument of growth and change. We avoid the term 'master plan', which connotes rigidity and finality, and use 'development plan', which implies orderly growth. Our aim is to define principles on which development can be based and which will allow, and even facilitate, changes of plan in future years."

-Peter Shepheard, Introduction to the Landscape Development Plan

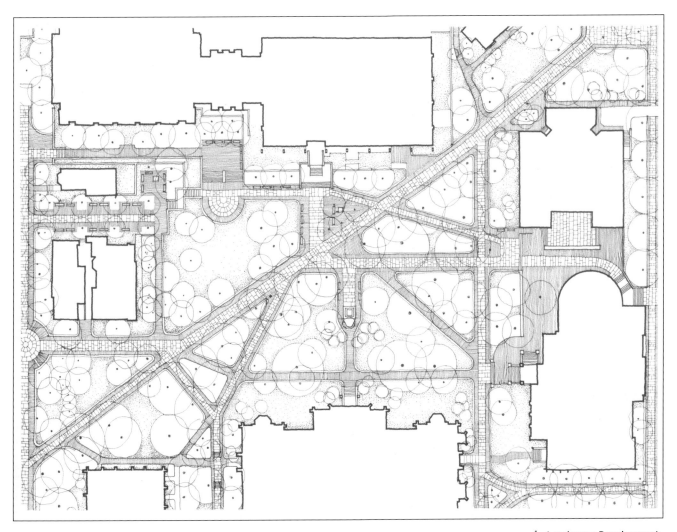

**Landscape Development Plan**

The plan transformed Penn's campus and gave direction for future development

1977

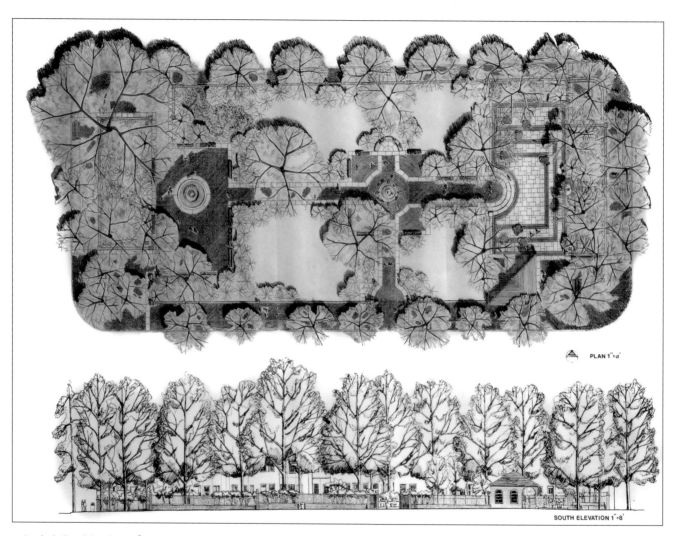

PLAN 1"=0'

SOUTH ELEVATION 1"=8'

**Lucinda Reed Sanders,
Studio 601**

Fitler Square, plan and
elevation, Bob Hanna,
studio professor

1979

"Landscape architects are the poetic stewards of the environment and humanity."

- Lucinda Reed Sanders, M.L.A. '81

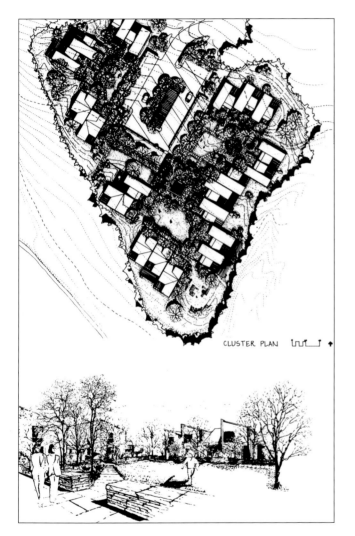

CLUSTER PLAN

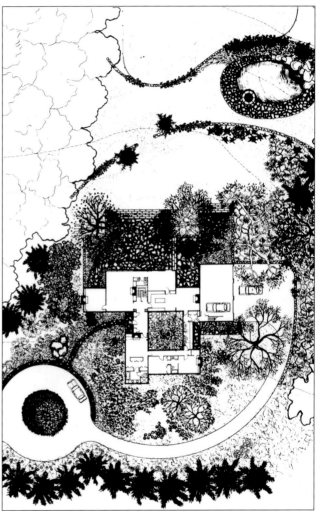

**Ed Hollander and
Alice Richardson,
Studio**

Jacobsburg Cluster
Housing and The
Horse Farm

1983

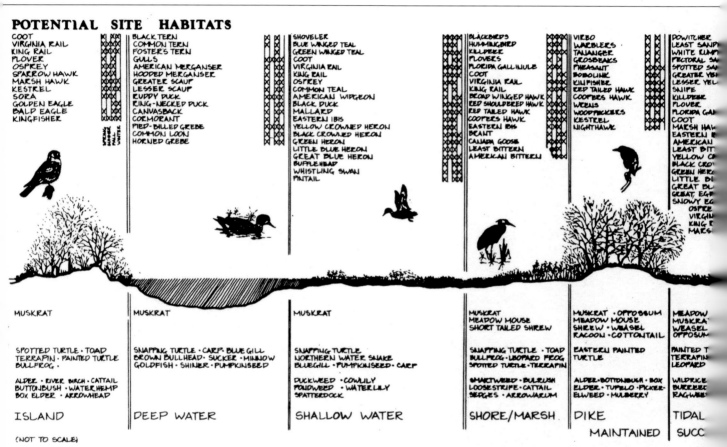

# POTENTIAL SITE HABITATS

**ISLAND** (NOT TO SCALE)

COOT
VIRGINIA RAIL
KING RAIL
PLOVER
OSPREY
SPARROW HAWK
MARSH HAWK
KESTREL
SORA
GOLDEN EAGLE
BALD EAGLE
KINGFISHER

MUSKRAT

SPOTTED TURTLE · TOAD
TERRAPIN · PAINTED TURTLE
BULLFROG

ALDER · RIVER BIRCH · CATTAIL
BUTTONBUSH · WATER HEMP
BOX ELDER · ARROWHEAD

**DEEP WATER**

BLACK TERN
COMMON TERN
FOSTER'S TERN
GULLS
AMERICAN MERGANSER
HOODED MERGANSER
GREATER SCAUP
LESSER SCAUP
RUDDY DUCK
RING-NECKED DUCK
CANVASBACK
CORMORANT
PIED-BILLED GREBE
COMMON LOON
HORNED GREBE

SPRING SUMMER FALL WINTER

MUSKRAT

SNAPPING TURTLE · CARP· BLUE GILL
BROWN BULLHEAD· SUCKER · MINNOW
GOLDFISH · SHINER · PUMPKINSEED

**SHALLOW WATER**

SHOVELER
BLUE WINGED TEAL
GREEN WINGED TEAL
COOT
VIRGINIA RAIL
KING RAIL
OSPREY
COMMON TEAL
AMERICAN WIDGEON
BLACK DUCK
MALLARD
EASTERN IBIS
YELLOW CROWNED HERON
BLACK CROWNED HERON
GREEN HERON
LITTLE BLUE HERON
GREAT BLUE HERON
BUFFLEHEAD
WHISTLING SWAN
PINTAIL

MUSKRAT

SNAPPING TURTLE
NORTHERN WATER SNAKE
BLUEGILL · PUMPKINSEED · CARP

DUCKWEED · COWLILY
PONDWEED · WATERLILY
SPATTERDOCK

**SHORE/MARSH**

BLACKBIRDS
HUMMINGBIRD
KILLDEER
PLOVERS
FLORIDA GALLINULE
COOT
VIRGINIA RAIL
KING RAIL
BROAD WINGED HAWK
RED SHOULDERED HAWK
RED TAILED HAWK
COOPERS HAWK
EASTERN IBIS
BRANT
CANADA GOOSE
LEAST BITTERN
AMERICAN BITTERN

MUSKRAT
MEADOW MOUSE
SHORT TAILED SHREW

SNAPPING TURTLE · TOAD
BULLFROG· LEOPARD FROG
SPOTTED TURTLE · TERRAPIN

SMARTWEED · BULRUSH
LOOSESTRIFE · CATTAIL
SEDGES · ARROWARUM

**DIKE — MAINTAINED**

VIREO
WARBLERS
TANAGER
GROSBEAKS
PHEASANT
BOBOLINK
KINGFISHER
RED TAILED HAWK
COOPERS HAWK
WRENS
WOODPECKERS
KESTREL
NIGHTHAWK

MUSKRAT · OPOSSUM
MEADOW MOUSE
SHREW · WEASEL
RACOON · COTTONTAIL

EASTERN PAINTED TURTLE

ALDER· BOTTONBUSH · BOX
ELDER · TUPELO · PICKER-
ELWEED · MULBERRY

**TIDAL SUCC...**

DOWITCHER
LEAST SANDP...
WHITE RUMP...
PECTORAL SAN...
SPOTTED SAN...
GREATER YEL...
LESSER YEL...
SNIPE
KILLDEER
PLOVER
FLORIDA GAL...
COOT
MARSH HAW...
EASTERN BI...
AMERICAN
LEAST BIT...
YELLOW CR...
BLACK CRO...
GREEN HER...
LITTLE BL...
GREAT BL...
GREAT EG...
SNOWY EG...
OSPREY
VIRGIN...
KING R...
MARS...

MEADOW...
MUSKRA...
WEASEL
OPOSSUM

PAINTED T...
TERRAPIN
LEOPARD

WILDRICE
BURREED
RAGWEE...

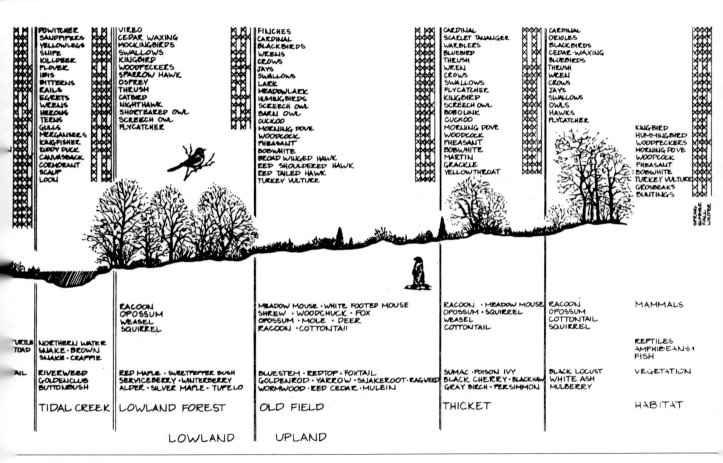

Ed Hollander, Studio

Pennypack Wildlife Refuge, potential site habitats

In 1984, McHarg set the stage for the future of the department with the re-introduction of computers. He had tried a computing system in 1969, but students were so turned off by the use of punchcards that he waited over a decade before bringing them back on a larger scale. The age of digital technology was welcomed at Penn, and computer analysis was soon a key part of the program. In 1986, as McHarg neared retirement age, the school selected Anne Whiston Spirn to succeed him as department chair. Spirn was a graduate of the program, and her work focused on the synthesis of nature and the city. She worked for five years at WMRT with McHarg and Juneja before leaving to teach at Harvard and to focus on writing her book, "The Granite Garden" in 1984, a prescient volume that recognized the importance of urban ecology for city design. Spirn continued to pursue her research through the establishment of the West Philadelphia Landscape Project in 1987, which utilized students and studios at Penn to explore how to rebuild communities and restore urban nature in synergistic ways, laying the groundwork for the city's landmark Green City, Clean Water program today. In 1990, McHarg became the first landscape architect to receive the National Medal of Arts.

# 1984-1993

Computers re-introduced in the Department of Landscape Architecture

Anne Whiston Spirn becomes chair of the department

McHarg receives National Medal of Arts
Lawrence Halprin gives life's work to Penn Architectural Archive

Patricia Conway becomes dean of the school

Dana Tomlin becomes interim chair of the department

| | |
|---|---|
| Human receives baboon heart<br>Apple launches Macintosh computer<br>Tschumi's Parc de la Villette<br>Spirn's "The Granite Garden" | 1984 |
| Hole in ozone layer discovered<br>US debt largest in world, $130 billion<br>8.1 magnitude earthquake in Mexico City<br>The SWA Group's William Square<br>Devall and Sessions' "Deep Ecology" | 1985 |
| Chernobyl reactor meltdown<br>Iran-Contra controversy<br>Space Shuttle Challenger accident | 1986 |
| Last CA condor trapped,<br>sent to zoo for breeding<br>World population, 5 billion<br>Van Gogh's "Irises" sells for $49 million | 1987 |
| George H. W. Bush elected US President<br>Gorbachev becomes last USSR President<br>Hawking's "A Brief History of Time"<br>Deconstructionism begins at MoMA<br>Best Picture "Rain Man" | 1988 |
| Exxon Valdez oil spill<br>6.9 magnitude earthquake in San Francisco<br>Berlin Wall falls<br>I.M Pei's Louvre renovation | 1989 |
| Nelson Mandela freed<br>Hubble telescope launched<br>Gulf War begins<br>Best Picture "Dances with Wolves" | 1990 |
| Gulf War ends<br>World Wide Web publicly launched<br>Cold War ends, USSR dissolves<br>Potsdamer Platz competition<br>Latz's Duisburg Nord | 1991 |
| Bill Clinton elected US President<br>Los Angeles riots over King beating<br>The Convention on Biological Diversity<br>West 8's Schouwbergplein<br>Olin's Bryant Park renovation | 1992 |
| Waco, Texas standoff<br>Congress of New Urbanism begins<br>MVVA's Mill Race Park<br>Best Picture "Schindler's List" | 1993 |

Sketching in Landscape
Drawing class

"There is reason to believe that the forthcoming year will be a landmark...the school has purchased computer hardware and software to the value of $500,000...The centerpiece of this hardware is an Intergraph II-751 CPU and three Intergraph Workstations.

The workstation has two screens, one color, the other black and white. Soil properties, depth to water tables can be compared to vegetation in a hydric to xeric gradiant. Geology can be displayed and compared to elevation, contours can be superimposed on either or both....There are limits to the number of students who can use a single workstation. However as there are three workstations...it should be possible to arrange instruction." -Ian McHarg, Letter to faculty

In the last two years, the Graduate School of Fine Arts has spent hundreds of thousands of dollars on computers, printers, and software. An investment of this magnitude is obviously significant and worth our attention. We at Penn In Ink decided to examine the impact the computer is making at the GSFA. The result is the following collection of four articles. Each reports on some aspect of how the computer is affecting and changing the curricula of three of the departments within the school.

The first article is an excerpt of an interview between Dr. John Radke, visiting professor in the Department of Landscape Architecture and Regional Planning last fall, and Matthew Miller, a LARP student. Radke's remarks present an overview of the history of the development of the computer, especially as it relates to the design professions. The second article highlights the activities of the students in the Department of Landscape Architecture and Regional Planning, the first users of the school's new CADD/CAM system. The third article focuses on the Department of City and Regional Planning, who first introduced computers to the GSFA in 1973. The last article examines the impact that computers are having in the Department of Architecture.

One thing we discovered in the process of our research is that computers mean different things to different people at the GSFA. To city planning and energy management students, computer analyses are an important part of their studies. To Ian McHarg, chairman of the Department of Landscape Architecture and Regional Planning (LARP), the computer enhances the ecological planning method he first outlined in his book Design With Nature. To William Glennie, a lecturer in the Department of Architecture, the computer means artificial intelligence. Glennie hopes to eventually research the possibility of using the computer not only for analysis but also for synthesis. To many students, the computer means skills that will help them be competitive in the job market. Whether one enjoys using them or not, computers are something one should know about, and know how to use. As Dr. John Radke says, "The computer is here today and it's here to stay."

# COMPUTERS:
## A Revolution at the GSFA?

*by Judy Coutts*

## Some Remarks by Radke
*An Interview by Matthew Miller*

Dr. John Radke spent the fall 1984 semester at Penn introducing some sixty LARP students to the intricacies of computer-aided design and cartographic work. Radke, from the Department of Geography, assisted Ian McHarg by establishing a workable Intergraph computer system. Radke's goal was to expand his students' understanding of the need and opportunities for computers in their chosen fields.

Radke talks here about the recent application of computers to the design professions, and the contributions he expects the CADD/CAM [computer-aided design/computer-aided mapping] system will make to the GSFA, and to the environmental design and planning professions.

"The computer has been a part of our technology for quite a while now, and it is here to stay. Unfortunately, before you advance this technology, there has to be a reason to prompt that advancement. Most of the time, advancement in computer technologies is military-related.

After computer industry researchers and designers saturated the military with computer technology, they sought other markets for a variety of applications, namely business. They turned it into a big electronic filing system. Now that the business world is nearing saturation with computer applications, the industry feels it is time to turn to the professions, such as law, medicine, design and planning.

Computer technology has taken more time to reach the architects, landscape architects, and planners because traditionally these have not been quantatative professions. Normally, a person within one of these professions would not learn a computer language to apply within their field. It wasn't until the last few years, that CADD-CAM systems have really progressed to a point where they are useful. Today, anyone can log on and do something useful right away! No longer do you need to take a programming course and waste your time learning to speak some language you don't appreciate. These systems are very 'operator-

Penn in Ink (University magazine) article on the Intergraph II-751 CPU's

1984

119

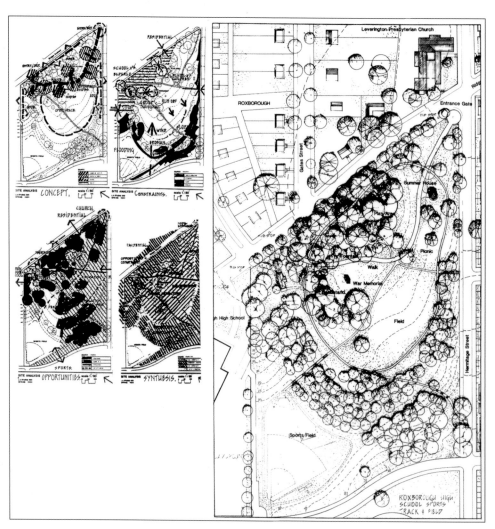

**Niall Kirkwood,
studio 502**

Gorgas Park restoration,
Bob Hanna,
studio professor

1985

"My years at Penn pursuing my degree were like a bridge, between one set of ideals and another. The modern and the decidedly post-modern." -William C. Hartman III, M.L.A. '89

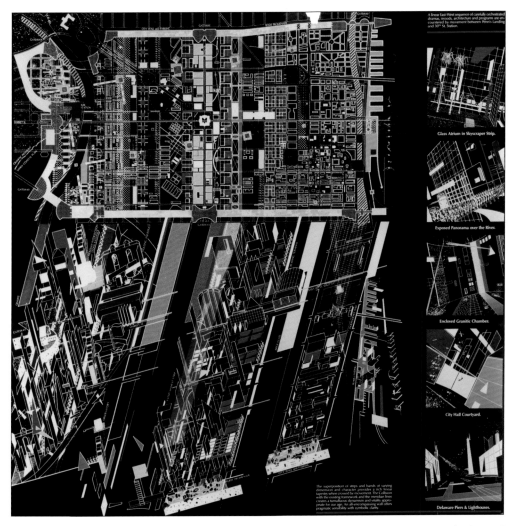

James Corner master thesis, "Philadelphia City"

1986

# Anne Whiston Spirn, M.L.A. '74

Anne Whiston Spirn
and Ian McHarg

Multi-colored maps of the Delaware River Basin (DRB), some many feet long, hung from the walls of the gallery on the ground floor of Meyerson Hall. It was September 1970, my first day of graduate school in Penn's Department of Landscape Architecture and Regional Planning. To the uninitiated, the maps on display, with no explanatory text, were bewildering and overwhelming. They documented research by students from the three preceding years, DRB I-III. We were to be DRB IV. Over the next three years, we learned to interpret and compose such maps and to employ them to read, plan and design the landscape. The biome, the physiographic region and the river basin were the context for our studies, augmented by an ethnographic approach to understanding and engaging the communities who lived there. Ours was the first class to work with anthropologists to study and map social and cultural processes and to explore their interplay with natural processes. We learned the fundamental importance to design of natural and social processes and how to work across multiple landscape scales from garden to region. Our class rode into Penn on the wave of the environmental movement: Earth Day and the Clean Air Act in 1970; the Clean Water and Coastal Zone Management acts in 1972. In 1970, the department's regional planning students way outnumbered the landscape architects, but, together, we were primed to change the world.

We landscape architects were not uncritical, however. Our first-year studio, which focused primarily on large-scale landscape analysis and planning, prompted a confrontation: "We want design." The sites for our second-year and third-year design studios were primarily rural and suburban: "What about the city?" Some of us pursued answers through independent courses. Heidi Cooke Shusterman and I, for example, did our thesis on Powelton

Village, in which we explored issues of nature, community and urban design. Earlier, when Heidi and I had tried to enroll in David Wallace's urban design studio, Ian strode into that studio, hauled us out and marched us back into his own class, which focused on planning for Woodlands New Community outside Houston, Texas. That turned out well for me. At the end of the semester, I went to Wallace McHarg Roberts & Todd (WMRT) to work on Woodlands. WMRT was an extension of the department; faculty and students shuttled between school and office; ideas were explored in classes, then applied in professional projects that advanced the profession, such as Woodlands, Sanibel and Pardisan. That synergy between school and practice is present in "Design with Nature", where McHarg uses both studio work and office projects to make his argument. The book was required reading in universities, and it was also an effective marketing tool for WMRT. During the recession of the mid 1970s, when most offices were laying off staff, "Design with Nature" was attracting new clients. By then, my work at WMRT was shifting from resorts and new towns to cities and urban regions. A project on the natural resources of the Toronto waterfront revealed the substantial information that existed about urban nature and demonstrated how right we students had been in our demand for an ecological urbanism.

Three years at Penn and five years at WMRT provided the foundation for my work ever since and raised questions that have driven my practice, research, and teaching. What is ecological design? What are its methods and historical precedents? What could urban ecological design be? My first book, "The Granite Garden: Urban Nature and Human Design" (1984) was an initial response, but it raised further questions. What are the poetics of ecological design? How can ecological design and planning address social injustice as well as environmental quality? My research and my courses at Harvard and Penn explored these questions. The answers I discovered, and my students' struggles to build a bridge between analysis and design, inspired my second book, "The Language of Landscape" (1998).

When I returned to Penn as chair in 1986, there were substantial challenges, including a declining student body and an enormous annual deficit. We had a wonderful faculty, including most of my own teachers, but the landscape architects among them, apart from Ian and myself, had busy professional practices and were teaching part-time. Others, such as Laurie Olin, had departed. Narendra Juneja, who had been so instrumental in shaping the curriculum since the early 1960s, had died in 1981, leaving a tremendous gap. The curriculum was sound in some areas, but ossified in others. The site for the second-year landscape architecture studio (LARP 602), for example, had not changed in fourteen years: "Please let me change that site. I'm sick of it!" John Collins pleaded. An inspiring teacher, his skills were confined by repetition. Maps presented in LARP 501, the first-year landscape planning studio, portrayed landscape as a set of static features without representing the natural and cultural processes that shaped those features. The maps resembled ones produced in the early 70s, despite Narendra's innovations of the mid-70s, where he had experimented with mapping and drawing methods that made vividly legible the connections between form and process. The task was to renew the curriculum in ways that strengthened the school's ecological design and planning tradition.

From 1986 to 1990, we introduced new courses in history, theory and representation, many of which were coordinated with studios, both required and elective. From 1986, I taught a module on "Poetics of Landscape" in LARP 501, in which students produced a graphic expression of the character of the site they had been analyzing from the perspective of science. A faculty search yielded three new hires for fall 1987: Kathryn Gleason (as assistant professor), James Corner (as full-time lecturer) and Gary Smith (as part-time adjunct). We also greatly expanded the size of the student body. The incoming class in fall 1987 was larger than the second- and third-year students combined. That class and the one that followed in fall 1988 were like a force of nature.

They demanded change, their energy propelled it and their accomplishments demonstrated the significance and value of the changes they inspired. The transformation in substance and style of drawing, for example, was dramatic. In fall 1988, students in Jim Corner's class in landscape representation produced extraordinary drawings and applied these new skills to their work for the 601 design studio, "The Garden." During an exhibit of student work, architecture students clustered around the drawings, fascinated. This marked the beginning of innovations in representation led by Corner and by Anuradha Mathur, when she was a student and, later, a faculty member. My own writing during this time ("Landscape Design Theory at Penn" and "The Poetics of City and Nature: Toward a New Aesthetic for Urban Design") laid out a vision for the landscape architecture curriculum, which charted the direction for changes from 1986 into the early 90s.

In 1988, Lawrence Halprin and I began a series of conversations about landscape architecture education. "You academics," Larry would say, "you are creating followers, not leaders." What would he advise? "First of all, every landscape architecture student should know how to design a building. Otherwise, they will always be subservient to architects. And they must be taught by a master." With this in mind, I invited the Australian architect Glenn Murcutt, a master of ecological design, to teach a studio. He challenged students to apply their understanding of natural processes to the design of a small building, and they produced extraordinary work. Glenn was appointed Adjunct Professor of Landscape Architecture in 1990, for a five-year term. Later, he would win the Alvar Aalto Medal and the Pritzker Prize, but it was in our department that he gave his first lectures and classes in the US. Out-of-town practitioners like Murcutt could not leave their practice for more than a few weeks, and there were no funds to pay for multiple trips back and forth. For several years, practitioners from around the country and the world taught a succession of three-week studios in the spring. During that time, they focused wholly on teaching, and, in order to eliminate the expenses of room and board, they stayed with my family. During Mario Sjetnan's stay we greatly expanded our collection of Mexican recipes and spices! While such out-of-towners spiced up studios and social life, local practitioners were an invaluable mainstay for semester-long and six-week studios, as well as other courses. Robert Hanna, Anthony Walmsley, Carol Franklin and Leslie Sauer continued to be influential, but, by 1986, they were teaching part-time, as was Peter Shepheard, who came from England to teach a six-week studio every fall and spring.

Meanwhile, my conversations with Halprin on landscape, process, form and education continued. Would he give a series of workshops at Penn? Yes, but only if he could have the students' full attention. In fall 1989, Larry spent several days at Penn and conducted an all-day workshop. Would he teach a studio? Later that year, he came back with a proposal that would cost the department nothing. There was a client whose project in Pennsylvania was too small for Halprin's office to undertake, but what if a group of students did so under his guidance, with the client paying all expenses, including Larry's fee? In spring 1990, Larry came to Penn at the beginning of the term for a field trip and to block out the semester's program, at the midpoint for a review, and at the end for a final review. Every week, the students sent him their work via Fed Ex; he reviewed it, then conferred with them the next day. The previous fall, Larry had broached the subject of a home for his archives. Over the course of his studio visits, we discussed this further, and Julia Converse, director of Penn's Architectural Archives, worked her magic. At the end of his studio's final review, Halprin expressed his delight with the students' work and announced his decision to give his archives to Penn.

Bringing the Halprin archives to Penn was a momentous occasion, but what about the archives of our own department? Returning to Penn in 1986 sparked my memory of the DRB maps that had hung in the gallery on my first day in 1970. Where were they? In a storage room on the third floor of Meyerson Hall, where drawings had been piled helter-skelter and were slated to be tossed out. Rummaging through piles several feet deep, I found them, along with maps and drawings of my class and others. A student catalogued them, and off they went into the archives. A few years later, when we ran out of filing space in the office, the director of University Archives accepted drawersful of files dating back to the department's early days into the university's collections. There were course syllabi, memos and notes of meetings in Ian's distinctive hand. Not all archives were on paper, however. Peter Shepheard was a living archive, as was Ian. In the early 1970s, Peter gave a lecture series each semester on "Light," "Water," "Plants," and similar topics. He agreed to repeat them in a 1987 public lecture series. The lectures packed the hall and were captured on video.

Ian emphasized invention over precedent. Apart from Anthony Walmsley's history class, the curriculum in landscape architecture at Penn from the 1960s through the 1970s was ahistorical, offering no introduction to, precedents for, or comparison among, alternative approaches to landscape design and planning. When he returned from sabbatical in 1987, Ian and I talked about the department's past and its future. Recordings of these conversations provided background for "Ian McHarg, Landscape Architecture, and Environmentalism," one of several essays that I wrote to document the contributions of Penn to design and planning history, theory and education. Other essays include "Renewing the Great Tradition: Urban Nature and Human Design, "The Authority of Nature: Conflict and Confusion in Landscape Architecture," and "Peter Shepheard and Teaching: To See, Tell, Design, and Build."

The renewal of the landscape architecture curriculum was well underway by 1988, but the regional planning program represented a much greater challenge. In 1986, there were only a handful of regional planning students, with an incoming class of three students. Regional planning (or landscape planning) was a major interest of many faculty. Ian and Nick Muhlenburg were still teaching in the department into the early 1990s, as were natural scientists Bob Giegengack, Arthur Johnson and James Thorne. In 1991, Dana Tomlin joined the faculty and established what would later become the Cartographic Modeling Laboratory. Despite this eminent faculty, the department's efforts to recruit more regional planners did not succeed. In 1992, when the school proposed that LARP and City and Regional Planning combine forces to offer a joint program in regional planning, Ian and Nick warned that this was a move designed to take away regional planning from our department. Unfortunately, they were right. Several years later, after my term as chairman, "regional planning" was stripped from the name of our department.

Ian's retirement in 1991 posed by far the most difficult challenge for me, personally. From the time he returned from sabbatical in 1988 until his mandatory retirement in 1991, Ian was a supportive partner and a positive force, and during that period, he taught twice as many courses than he had while he had been chairman. At the time, retirement at age 70 was mandated by federal law. I had managed to negotiate half-time teaching salary for him, but not full-time (the other half would have swallowed the department's discretionary budget for part-time teaching, which we relied on to staff studios and other required courses). Ian's anger and despair at the forced retirement were grievous; they affected the entire department and intensified conflicts among faculty about the nature of ecological design.

When I arrived at Penn in 1986, Ian asked if I planned to turn the department into a program on urban ecology. "No," I laughed. But, in 1987, I did embark on an ambitious action research program – the West Philadelphia Landscape Project (WPLP) – which, for the past quarter century, has integrated all that I learned at Penn and has been a vehicle for teaching others about landscape literacy and ecological design and planning. WPLP deals with vexing problems that are usually treated separately, such as vacant urban land, polluted water and troubled public schools, and views them, instead, as opportunities for integrated solutions rather than disconnected liabilities. It combines top-down and bottom-up approaches, involving dozens of organizations and hundreds of individuals, including groups who rarely work together such as inner-city residents, middle-school children, university students, and municipal water engineers. A key proposal of the project is to manage the watershed as part of a broad approach to improving regional water quality and as a strategy to secure funds to rebuild inner-city neighborhoods. From 1987-2000, WPLP employed dozens of Penn students as research assistants and in studios and workshops; since 2000, it has involved students at MIT and Harvard. Students have explored innovative strategies for water management, created new visions for Mill Creek's buried floodplain and presented their ideas to the city, which inspired and contributed to the revolution in water-quality management represented by Philadelphia's billion-dollar "green" infrastructure project, Green City, Clean Water. "Restoring Mill Creek: Landscape Literacy, Environmental Justice, and City Planning and Design" tells part of this story. The ongoing work continues to bring me back to Philadelphia and keeps me mindful of the debt I owe to my teachers, colleagues and former students at Penn.

Book covers,
Anne Whiston Spirn

# Ignacio F. Bunster-Ossa, M.L.A. '79 on Anne Whiston Spirn, M.L.A. '74

The world today has become urbanized. Cities are now humanity's habitat of choice. How this habitat functions ecologically to the benefit of people and wildlife cannot be overstated as a concern for urban planners and designers. To this central question, the contribution of Anne Whiston Spirn stands as a monument; for its far-reaching scope, to be sure; but more important as a marker, a guidepost for the profession to follow. When "The Granite Garden" was published in 1984, the United States was experiencing massive suburbanization. Much of this development was enabled by environmental regulations that protected sensitive natural resources, such as wetlands. The effect was the creation of a 'green' development mosaic that sustained for millions of home buyers the perception that a healthy living environment could only exist away from urban centers. The title of Anne's book alone redirected the perception towards core urban areas, providing a critical, as well as technical, understanding of how cities could—and should—become as healthy as any exurban locale. In doing so, Anne pointed the way towards a sustainable future long before sustainability entered the professional lexicon. Her ideas about urban ecology made Anne the recipient of the Cosmos Prize, the only landscape architect thus far to merit such recognition. "The Granite Garden" has since served as a foundation for new vital strands of practice, such as Landscape Urbanism.

Of equal, if not greater value, has been Anne's focus upon the social standing of urban areas, specifically as related to the oft ignored relationship between urban change and community well-being. The West Philadelphia Landscape Project, to which Anne has dedicated more than two decades of study, stands as a unique and essential example. The work tracks the historical change of an impoverished watershed, shedding light on the human and economic impacts stemming from an ignored ecology— but also the promise embedded in its potential restoration. Anne's work in West Philadelphia served to highlight for city officials the need to consider the management of stormwater as a vital ecological resource and positive source of community health. The City of Philadelphia Division of Watersheds took note of Anne's work and consulted with her, leading ultimately to the preparation and adoption of the globally acclaimed Clean City/Green Water program—the nation's first to bank heavily on green infrastructure to meet federal water quality mandates. As a planner and landscape architect, Anne was preoccupied with the ecological health of cities and well-being of disadvantaged communities at a time when prominent academics and practitioners were not. Her emphasis on the poetics of design as an integral aspect of urban health, too, preceded mainstream practice. This was the focus of her second master work, "The Language of Landscape." Taken together as a related body of work, "The Granite Garden", The West Philadelphia Landscape Project and "The Language of Landscape" have no equal in the value and significance to the city-building professions.

In the late 1980's, Spirn, Corner and others began to more deeply explore representation and process, in studios, elective courses and in their own practices. They challenged students to rethink and redefine landscape drawing.

Alan Berger,
Representation and
Landscape

1988

"Drawing has the same relationship to landscape and architectural design as writing has to poetry and that mathematics has to physics." - Course Description, Drawing: Design & Form, James Corner

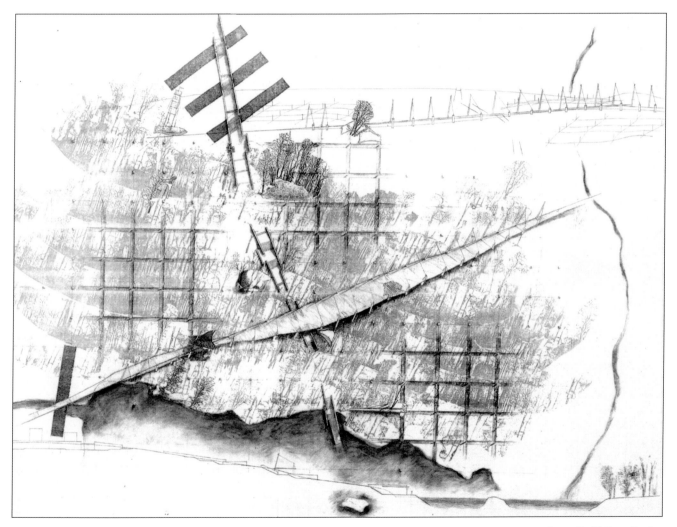

**Anuradha Mathur, Studio**

Winterthur Garden
and Estate

1990

During Spirn's tenure, she brought a number of notable landscape architects and architects to teach at the department, such as Lawrence Halprin and Glenn Murcutt.

While at Penn, Halprin was so impressed with the quality of the architectural archive, that in 1990 he agreed to donate his entire life's work to the University upon his death.

Lawrence Halprin, Anne Whiston Spirn and Paul Shepheard, Sir Peter Shepheard's son, at Sea Ranch, CA

This was a monumental moment for the school. Not only is Halprin legendary in the field of landsacpe architecture, but his body of work is unprecedented in size.

His donation to the archive consisted of 800 linear feet of records; 45,000 drawings; 141 notebooks; 155,000 color slides; 60,000 photographic images; and dozens of models, scrapbooks and films.

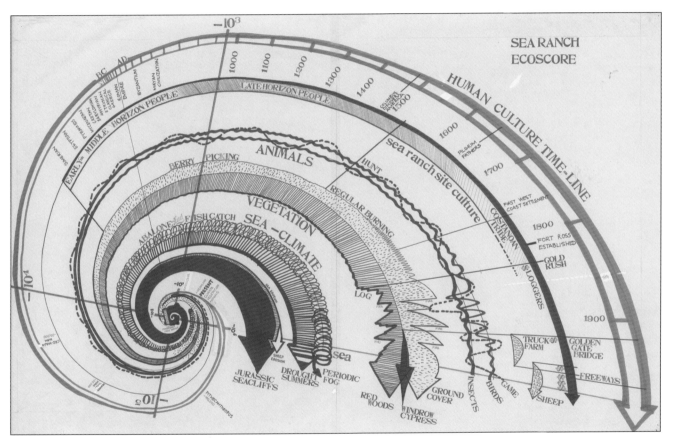

**Sea Ranch Ecoscore**

Halprin's famed analysis of the Sea Ranch community along the north coast of California

1990

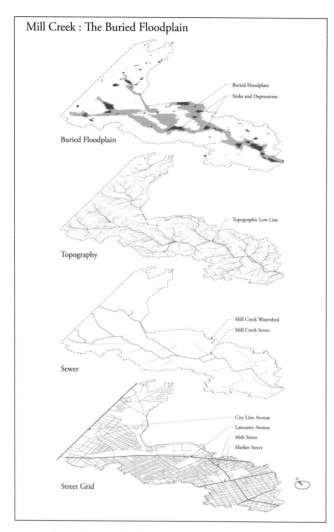

**Mill Creek : The Buried Floodplain**

Buried Floodplain

Buried Floodplain
Sinks and Depressions

Topography

Topographic Low Line

Sewer

Mill Creek Watershed
Mill Creek Sewer

Street Grid

City Line Avenue
Lancaster Avenue
46th Street
Market Street

**Analysis maps for
West Philadelphia
Landscape Project**

In 1987, Spirn launched The West Philadelphia Landscape Project (WPLP), "a landmark of urban design and design education, environmental sustainability and community engagement".

-West Philadelphia Landscape Project, Anne Whiston Spirn

In 1991, Spirn published the research, design and analysis of the project, in hopes of promoting large scale landscape planning for both stormwater mitigation and also as a community development tool. WPLP promotes vacant lot reclamation through community design build efforts and has proved, over a 25 year period, the impacts that lot improvements can have on both city infrastructure and community cohesion and identity. Philadelphia's landmark Green City, Clean Water program is based on the work of WPLP, and Spirn continues to develop the project through studios and research at MIT.

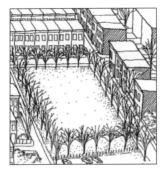

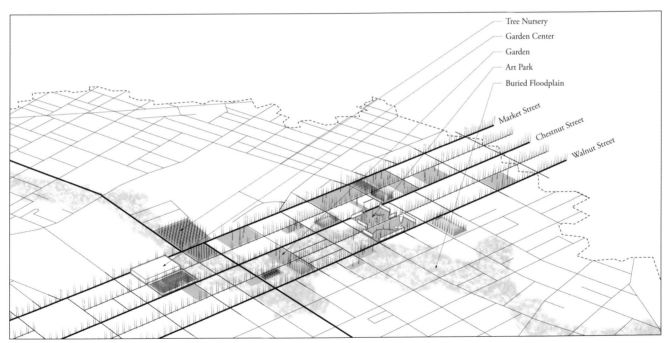

Tree Nursery
Garden Center
Garden
Art Park
Buried Floodplain
Market Street
Chestnut Street
Walnut Street

Renderings and plan
for West Philadelphia
Landscape Project

1991

1994 saw a shift as Spirn became the Director of the Urban Studies Program at Penn and John Dixon Hunt, who brought a reputation as perhaps the world's leading theorist and historian of landscape architecture, became chair of the department. Between 1994 and 1999, under Hunt's leadership, the faculty began significant explorations in the collaboration between design and theory, placing the school at the forefront of critical design thinking. In 2000, James Corner was named the new chair of the Department. Under his leadership and tenure, the department continued to advance contemporary ideas in theory, with renewed emphasis on ecology, technology, digital media and urbanism. Both Hunt and Corner's commitment to advancing design dialogue across the international community has established the department as a center of global discourse and practice. Also in 2000, McHarg received the renowned Japan Prize in planning and Hunt was appointed as Chevalier des Arts et des Lettres in France. In 2001, Spirn was awarded the prestigious International Cosmos Prize for a lifetime of ecological achievement. In 2003, as a reflection of the broader scope of the school, the name was changed from Graduate School of Fine Arts to simply School of Design.

# 1994-2003

John Dixon Hunt becomes chair of the department

Patricia Conway resigns as dean of the school

Malcolm Campbell becomes interim dean

Gary Hack becomes dean of the school

James Corner becomes chair of the department

McHarg receives the Japan Prize

Hunt appointed as Chevalier des Arts

Spirn awarded the Cosmos Prize

Graduate School of Fine Arts becomes School of Design

| | |
|---|---|
| **Mandela elected president of South Africa** | **1994** |
| **Magnitude 6.7 earthquake in Los Angeles** | |
| Hunt's "Gardens and the Picturesque" | |
| Miralles and Pinós' Igualda Cemetery | |
| Best Picture "Forrest Gump" | |
| **Oklahoma City bombing** | **1995** |
| **O.J. Simpson trial** | |
| **Fighting escalates in Bosnia & Croatia** | |
| Lin's Wave Field | |
| Best Picture "Braveheart" | |
| **Outbreak of Mad Cow disease** | **1996** |
| **First cloned sheep "Dolly"** | |
| **Taliban seize Kabul** | |
| Corner's "Taking Measure Across the American Landscape" | |
| **Kyoto protocol signed** | **1997** |
| **Hong Kong reverts to China** | |
| Gehry's Guggenheim Bilbao | |
| Halprin's FDR Memorial | |
| Best Picture "Titanic" | |
| **Lewinsky scandal, Clinton impeachment trial** | **1998** |
| **India and Pakistan do nuclear tests** | |
| Spirn's "The Language of Landscape" | |
| Irwin's Getty Central Garden | |
| "Citizen Kane" nominated best film ever | |
| **Columbine High School shooting** | **1999** |
| **Y2K crisis** | |
| **World population, 6 billion** | |
| Corner's "Recovering Landscape" | |
| Downsview Park competition | |
| **George W. Bush elected US President** | **2000** |
| **Human genome deciphered** | |
| Olin's "Across the Open Field" | |
| FOA's Yokohama Terminal | |
| Schwartz's Exchange Square | |
| **September 11th attacks on World Trade Center** | **2001** |
| **War in Afghanistan begins** | |
| Mathur and da Cunha's "Mississippi Floods" | |
| Weller/Sitta's "Garden of Australian Dreams" | |
| Fresh Kills competition | |
| **Department of Homeland Security created** | **2002** |
| **Enron scandal** | |
| Best Picture "Chicago" | |
| **Space Shuttle Columbia accident** | **2003** |
| **Iraq War begins** | |
| **Oldest light in the Universe 'captured'** | |
| Best Picture "The Lord of the Rings" | |

Model making for
Studio 501

# John Dixon Hunt

# Reflection

As I assumed the chairmanship, what seemed useful
was to ensure that there was a wider intellectual range,
with more historical and theoretical emphasis (history of
ideas, especially). I was also keen to see that more P.h.D.
work was done, and that as a school we developed good
contacts with other schools. Landscape architecture
requires both a detailed and professional approach
to design with its related pragmatic needs (what any
accreditation requires); yet it also needs to situate itself in
a culture where it can be seen and understood by others
outside the field. There are some uncertainties about
where the profession wants to go, and more superficially,
what it wants to call itself; it needs, and is gaining, a
considerable role in the urban design field. It still needs to
explain itself better for audiences beyond the profession,
for landscape architecture must learn to speak to a wider,
non-professional audience: this is hard, as many within the
profession want (perhaps understandably) to talk only to
themselves and for their greater academic advancement.
What I enjoyed at Penn as a historian was getting to
know the scope and dynamics of the field, and learning to
situate myself therein; encouraging a few (too few, alas)
P.h.D.s in the field, including at least one from art history;
helping to see landscape architecture as a topic that had
wider repercussions beyond the department, with better
contacts in architecture, historical preservation and fine
arts, and myself belonging to groups in comparative
literature, italian studies and art history.

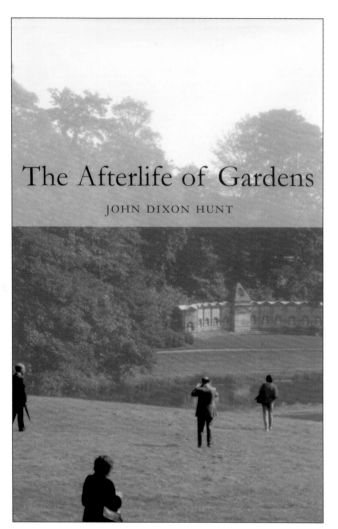

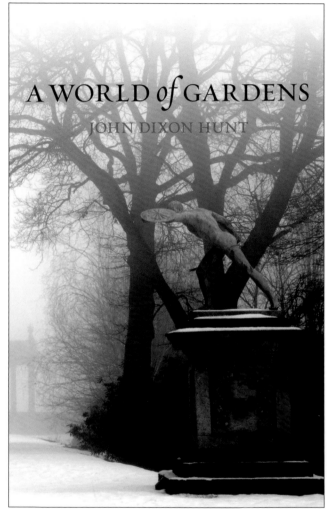

Book covers,
John Dixon Hunt

# James Corner on John Dixon Hunt

"You have constructed an almost unassailable argument that the specificity of sites lies at the very core of any significant works of landscape architecture. In this vein, you have elaborated on key concepts such as the 'genius of the place,' 'reading and writing the site,' 'place-making as an art of milieu,' 'site mediation,' and the nesting of 'three natures' wherein the garden is a concentration and focusing of its larger surroundings. A close reading of a particular site's specific attributes—its history, its various representations, its context and its potentials—conspires to inform a new project that is in some way an intensification and enrichment of place. You have written, 'The garden will contain a concentration of the qualities and affects of the larger locality.' Every site is unique, an accumulation of local forces over time, and so, you argue, any significant design response must in some way interpret, extend and amplify this potential within its specific context. Averse to universal and stylistic approaches to design, you quite rightly demand inventive originality with regard to specific circumstance.

The combination of physical, material places with cultural ideas points to the unity of theory with practice, of design with reception, of experience with intellect, all dialogues that we strive for in the best of our work. That such experiences might also haunt our imaginations is perhaps the highest calling of art, and in gardens, as John has so eloquently taught us, we might find the greatest perfections." - Speech on the occasion of John Dixon Hunt's retirement

In 1996, Spirn introduced a new element into her studios, requiring all of her students to be proficient in GIS and web authoring. All work was published online, creating a database of solutions in stormwater management that were easily accessible to those outside of the school.

**Eric Husta and Steven Sattler, Studio 601**

Anne Whiston Spirn, studio professor

**Eric Husta and Steven Sattler, Studio 601**

Anne Whiston Spirn, studio professor

1996

Throughout the late 1990's, Hunt encouraged professors and lecturers to broadly define the field of landscape architecture. Spirn, along with Hanna, continued explorations in urban processes, while Franklin and Sauer brought their experience in practice to real world studio problems. Corner consistently blurred the lines in his studios between landscape and urbanism, at one point asking students to redesign all of Philadelphia, and new professors such as Anuradha Mathur and Dilip da Cunha pushed the boundaries of representation and theory.

Hunt also brought internationally renowned designers such as Paolo Bürgi, Barnard Lassus and Peter Latz to the department, supporting them and others in exploring studio problems around the world.

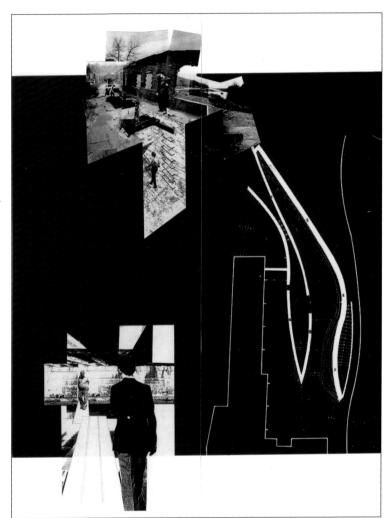

Jonathan Reo, Studio 701 and Charles Neer, Eliza Booth, Mark Meagher, Landscape Drawing

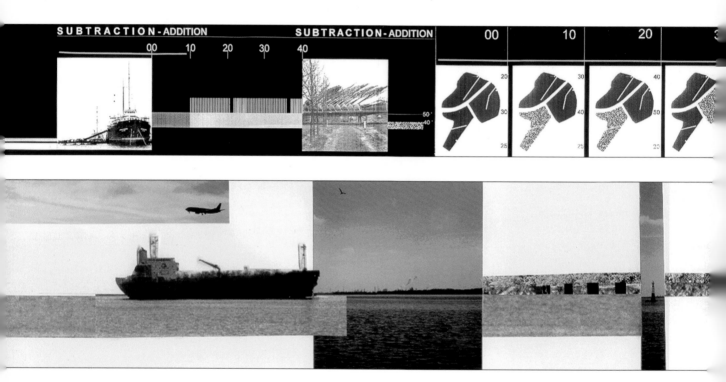

SUBTRACTION-ADDITION

SUBTRACTION-ADDITION

00 10 20 30 40

00 10 20 3

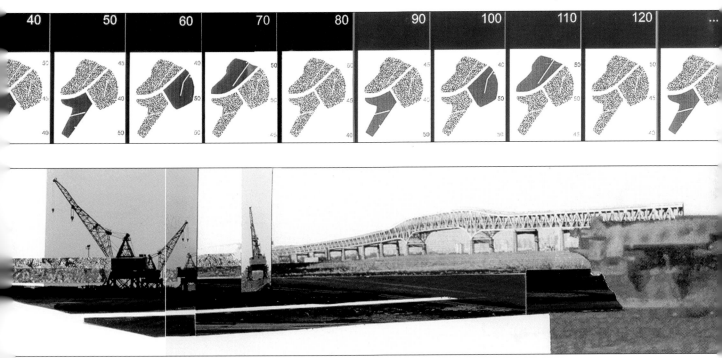

Patricia Uribe, Studio 602

1999

153

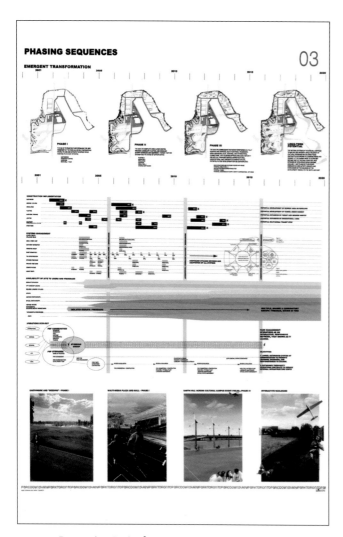

Downsview Park
competition, Stan Allen
with James Corner
Field Operations

In 1999, Corner partnered with Stan Allen on a competition entry for Downsview Park Toronto. Many viewed the competition as a turning point for the design of urban parks. All five finalists shared a theme of frameworks that allowed the site to evolve over time. The entries are often pointed to as examples of landscape urbanism.

Shortly thereafter, Corner formed Field Operations and in 2001 submitted a proposal for the Fresh Kills competition, a redevelopment of a former landfill site on Staten Island. The competition entry was revolutionary in its thinking, proposing a thirty year plan to transform a barren wasteland of garbage into a system of creeks, wetlands and meadows.

Field Operations has since grown to become an international practice with many Penn alumni, including principals Tatiana Choulika (M.L.A. '88), Lisa Switkin (M.L.A. '00), Karen Tamir (M.L.A. '00), Hong Zhou (M.L.A. '01), Sarah Weidner Astheimer (M.L.A. '04), Tsutomu Bessho (M.L.A. '05) and Isabel Castilla (M.L.A. '07).

1999

Fresh Kills competition
rendering, James Corner
Field Operations

2001

# James Corner, MLA '86

I arrived at Penn Design (then the Graduate School of Fine Arts) nearly 30 years ago—August 1984. The great man, Ian McHarg himself, picked me up at the airport in his truck and dropped me at my new digs. I was impressed with McHarg's generosity of spirit and his absolute dedication to the field and to the school.  As I then became immersed in the Masters program, McHarg continued to astound with his larger-than-life presence, passionate energy and vision. I must have read "Design with Nature" five or six times that first year! McHarg had inaugurated a whole new landscape project, one that broached all scales and disciplines.

During that time though, toward the end of McHarg's long tenure as chair, the program seemed to be losing steam; more the repetition of an over-rehearsed ideology and curriculum that was becoming dogmatic and formulaic. The imagination and impetus that originally propelled McHarg's project had somehow calcified or become exhausted. The environmental moral imperative remained the same, but the means and methods limited critical innovation and creativity.

After McHarg's amazing 30 year run as chair, he stepped down and was replaced by Anne Whiston Spirn in 1986. She wanted to change things, focus more on design, and bring criticism and poetics in to balance the science.  She hired me to teach drawing, representation and core design studios. It was daring of her to do so as I had earned a bit of a reputation for being too experimental, too avant-garde or too much of an instigator. I certainly had the naïveté of youth, but also the drive to help advance design creativity, and Anne was a strong supporter. Some of those early years were extremely creative and significant for me and for the department more broadly. Visual representation, as well as imaging as a source of creativity, became my main interest, together with design theory and criticism. This work appeared esoteric and marginal to some of the older

McHargians, who could not see the connection between drawing, collage, narrative and cultural critique with saving the environment through more rational means. And they were right—there was a quite distinct disconnect. Yet I still believed there could be a union forged between the more objective, positivist approach and the subjective, experiential approach. I was searching for a new landscape project that reconciled McHarg with the poetic and the imaginative.

In 1994, John Dixon Hunt was recruited as the new chair. This was a radical departure from McHarg's environmental scientism and Spirn's concern for process and poetics. Hunt represented history, thought, criticism and theory— concerns that were absolutely critical to the field at that juncture in time, and, in my view, completely necessary to not only refresh the field and the school but to also extend and expand the programs of McHarg and Spirn in new directions. Anuradha Mathur and I took the lead with Hunt to forge a radically new curriculum structure, and sought to unite design with all of the intellectual and technical aspects surrounding that endeavor. It was a heady time, with a sense of new wind in the sails. We were finally beginning to achieve that much-sought-after synthesis between the rational and the imaginative projects. Student design work was exemplary, and new directions with landscape cartography, landscape infrastructure and landscape urbanism were born. Hunt's emphasis on consistent and clear lines of verbal articulation and argument were incredibly powerful in developing stronger thought and ideation processes as well as skills with communication and dialogue—all key to assuming professional leadership roles.

During my own tenure as chair, beginning in 2000, I wanted to continue many of the good things we had developed over the past few years, and place an even greater focus even upon design, digital media and urbanism. Urban design in particular became a focus simply because there was such a desperate need to re-think approaches toward urbanism given global growth and rapid processes of urbanization. Landscape provided not only a good lens for looking at urbanization, but also a good set of tools and techniques to take on the complexly layered medium of the city—including some revamped tools from McHarg. If Penn's landscape architects could work not only with traditional forms of landscape and public space, but also become sufficiently competent to help orchestrate the complex ecologies of the city, including built urban form and infrastructure, then perhaps there might be an even greater scope and relevance for the field more broadly. In this regard, it was important to me that we encourage and teach leadership skills, with all of the initiative and energy that requires, as well as broaching the challenges of working internationally, in geographies and contexts quite different to our own. We took students to places where a landscape approach to urbanism might be especially applicable in the context of rapid urbanization and radical cultural shifts—places such as Rio de Janiero, Beijing, Mumbai, Caracas and Morrocco—and we looked at other more developed cities for their various design achievements and radical urban overhauls—Barcelona, Paris, London and Copenhagen, for example. I like to think that the past 15 or so years at Penn has produced some of our most sophisticated graduates— skilled in design, critically aware of broader historical and current cultural issues, technically proficient, and professionally ambitious with regard to the kind of work they want to be a part of.

Now, nearly 100 years since the program's inception, Richard Weller has assumed the chair and promises yet another distinctive and important chapter in our story— one confronting global urbanization, ecological challenges and cultural difference, as well as charting new directions for design and critical agendas. I am excited about the next decade and beyond at Penn. Weller is the perfect complement and leader for our particular faculty, and together we offer sufficient diversity of interest and approach, as well as shared focus and purpose. Looking forward, I believe it is important to continue the main strengths that have always characterized our program. Irrespective of differing paradigms, approach and ideology, our program has always been adventurous, ambitious, pioneering, innovative and productive. We have also been remarkably multi-disciplinary—learning not only from closely related subjects such as ecology, geography, history, engineering, urban planning, architecture and painting, but also from less obvious disciplines such as literature, film, anthropology, cultural criticism, biology and sociology. At the same time, we are careful to pay attention to the content of our own discipline—its history, ideas, design techniques, construction and technology. We have always been committed ultimately to practice, to making a difference in how the world is shaped, made and lived.

In all of this, however, there is one ingredient that I feel we need to not forget. Indeed, this may be the one thing we need to better understand and nurture. For lack of a better term, I would call this the landscape imagination, or more precisely, practices of the imagination. That is, the capacity to imagine landscape in all of its full plenitude and richness, and at the same time the capacity to imagine and project it otherwise. As a medium, landscape (like its corollary 'nature') can be filled with habits and conventions—many of them useful and relevant, but others restrictive and limited. When confronted with any new project, the main limiting factor is our own imagination. And if not the imagination per-se, then the capacity to actually project that vision forward into a built and performative reality is almost certainly a limit. Whether ecology, history, place-making, sustainability or urbanism—or whatever one's particular focus might be—the main challenge with the landscape medium lies not only in technical and comprehensive proficiency, but also with broader imaginative practices— practices that extend a project beyond its already known limits.

Design schools and studios are perhaps the best place we have for exploring the landscape imagination and for developing new ideas, techniques, procedures and practices that might body forth new forms of landscape project; but not only new forms—new consequences, effects and programs. Penn's landscape project has a great legacy, and has taken many guises over the years, but now is the time to look forward and help to evolve that project into something of even greater scope, efficacy and imaginative depth.

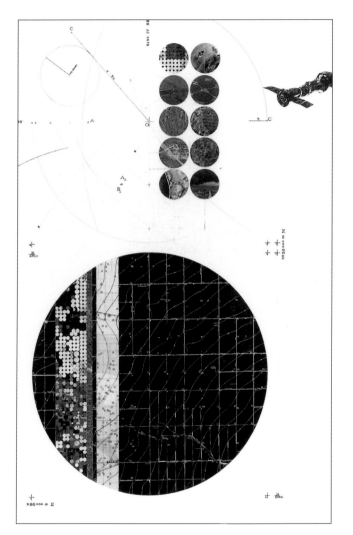

Images from 'Taking Measure Across the American Landscape'

# Richard Weller on James Corner

James Corner's intellectual impact began in the early 1990s with two essays in Landscape Journal. "Discourse on Theory 1: Sounding the Depths—Origins, Theory and Representation" provided a useful cursory history of the philosophy of science as a way of contextualising landscape architecture's own narratives. "Discourse on Theory 2: Three Tyrannies of Contemporary Theory and the Alternative of Hermeneutics" went on to outline a contemporary philosophy of landscape design based on, and borrowing from, hermeneutics, the study of textual interpretation. These papers brought together wide ranging interests in how history, art, design method and poetics related to landscape architecture toward the close of the 20th century. They crystalized some of the deepest (and largely repressed) artistic and intellectual ambitions of landscape architecture at the time.

Then in order to 'see' the landscape McHarg had implored us to 'steward', Corner takes flight with the celebrated aerial photographer, Alex Maclean. In the resultant "Taking Measures Across the American Landscape" (1996), he documents a beguiling beauty in the sprawling, denatured world below and starts making his own maps from aerial images and associated fragments of data. In a related essay "The Agency of Mapping: Speculation, Critique and Invention" (1999) he explains that instead of the accepted landscape architectural formula that defers design until after the data is collected, the entire process of collecting, assembling and inter-relating data, is creative.

Around the same time in a daring and wide ranging essay entitled "Ecology and Landscape as Agents of Creativity", he turns to the question that has been so central to Penn's intellectual life; how ecology and creativity can mutually inform the design process. Corner's answer is that human creativity and ecosystems share the same tendency toward the increased "differentiation, freedom, and richness of a diversely interacting whole". With this he moves beyond judgement over the loss of nature and opens to a landscape of coevolving systems requiring design intelligence so as to maximize both cultural and ecological potential.

In his edited volume "Recovering Landscapes" (1999)—a book which did much to reaffirm landscape architecture as a serious cultural endeavor—his frustration with landscape's prelapsarian inclinations and its infrastructural impotence is palpable. To alter this he embraces contemporary urbanism and through various essays in the late 90's and early 2000s he explains ways in which landscape architecture could play a more powerful role in the making of the city.

In the vast and disorienting atmosphere of post modern thought James Corner's writings served as a lightning rod for the discipline. Corner, I think uniquely, seemed to be able to discuss the landscape architectural project through, and not in spite of the broader cultural milieu of postmodern thought. Without banging on the empty drum of stewardship and sustainability, he could nonetheless present the landscape project in exalted terms, inspiring a generation of students to be more erudite, more artful and more ambitious.

-Excerpt from "Wordscape: The Writings of James Corner in Theory and Practice in The Landscape Imagination." James Corner and and Alison Hirsch, J. Princeton Architectural Press

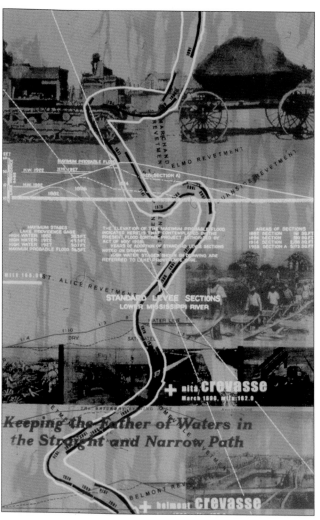

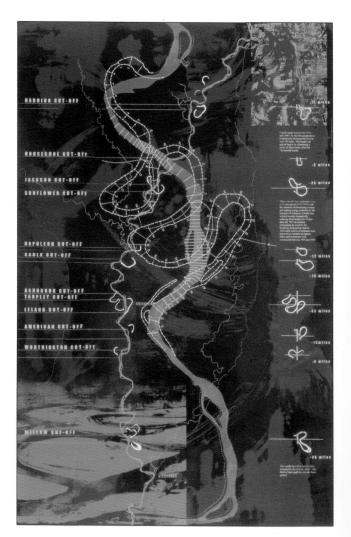

Images from
"Mississippi Floods"

In 2001, professors Mathur and da Cunha released "Mississippi Floods: Designing a Shifting Landscape", a synthesis of eight years spent explored the Mississippi River, through maps and photographs, in stories and by canoe. They questioned how representation of the river has defined our perception of it, and how new ways of seeing could change our relationship to our environment. This ideology is also the basis of their teachings at Penn.

"The environment is fast ceasing to be just our 'surrounds' that bears the impact of human activity and manifest such impact in what are called 'environmental/ecological problems' that preoccupy designers and planners. It is increasingly becoming a 'place of debate', an arena for critiquing, explaining, interpreting and inventing nature."

-Nature and Environment, Course outline, Dilip da Cunha

**Mathur and da Cunha**

2001

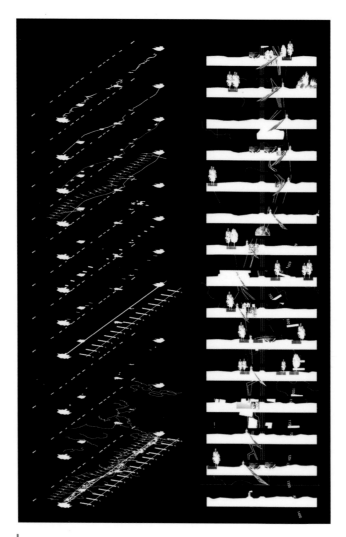

Shian-Po Liao,
Studio 602

Chih-Ciun (Grace) Ling,
Studio 701

2001

Ellen Neises, Studio 702

Corner, a prolific writer, designer and educator, took the department and the profession to new heights during his time as chair. He surrounded himself with a staff of likeminded urbanists and thinkers that continue to set the tone of the department today. 2007 was a tumultuous year as the financial crisis caused a massive decline in construction projects, leaving many firms to severely cut back or shutter entirely. In 2008, Marilyn Jordan Taylor became dean of the School of Design. Taylor established herself through a 35-year career at Skidmore Owings & Merrill LLP, where she was the first woman to serve as chair of the firm. She was also the first architect and the first woman to serve as chair of the Urban Land Institute, a non-profit research and educational institution. In 2010, the Sixth European Biennial unanimously named the department as the best program in landscape architecture in the world, based on the dynamic nature of the problems posed in the studios and the breadth of design work in scale, scope and location. Corner officially stepped down as department chair in December 2012, leaving a century of landscape design and education in the hands of his successor, Richard Weller.

# 2004-2013

Marilyn Jordan Taylor
becomes dean of
the school

Barcelona Biennial
selects department
as best landscape
program in the world

Richard Weller
becomes chair of
the department

Laurie Olin receives
National Medal of
the Arts

**Facebook publicly launched**
**Massachusetts becomes first**
**state to legalize gay marriage**
Hunt's "The Afterlife of Gardens"
Gustafson Guthrie Nichol Ltd, Piet Oudolf
and Robert Israel's Lurie Garden

2004

**IRA announces end to hostilities**
**Hurricane Katrina disaster**
**Magnitude 7.6 earthquake in Pakistan**
Mathur and daCunha's "Deccan Traverses"
Weller's "Room 4.1.3"
Smith's MoMA Roof Garden

2005

**Pluto reclassified as a dwarf planet**
Foster and Partners' Masdar City
JCFO's High Line
MVVA's Teardrop Park
West 8's Toronto Waterfront

2006

**Pelosi, first female speaker of the house**
**Great Recession begins**
MVVA's Boston Children's Museum
Weiss/Manfredi's Olympic Sculpture Park

2007

**Barack Obama elected US President**
**Castro steps down**
Turenscape's Red Ribbon Park
MVDRV's Logroño Montecorvo Eco City
Beijing Olympics

2008

**Swine flu epidemic**
**Michael Jackson dies**
**General Motors files for bankruptcy**
Mathur and da Cunha's "Soak"
Best Picture "The Hurt Locker"

2009

**Volcano in Iceland erupts**
**Deepwater Horizon oil spill,**
**worst spill in history**
Picasso painting sells for $106.5 million
Scape's Oyster-tecture
Minneapolis Riverfront Competition

2010

**US withdraws from Iraq**
**8.9 magnitude earthquake/tsunami in Japan**
**World population, 7 billion**
Halprin's "A Life Spent Changing Places"
JCFO's Race Street Pier
OLIN's Central Delaware Riverfront Plan

2011

**Hurricane Sandy disaster**
**"Curiosity" lands on Mars**
Hunt's "A World of Gardens"
Turenscape's Qunli Stormwater Park
London Olympics

2012

**Boston Marathon bombing**
**DOMA struck down, same sex**
**couples granted federal rights**
West 8's Governor's Island

2013

Final reviews, critics
and audience

"I remember approaching Corner as an architecture student who just realized that landscape architecture was what I was interested in. He said that architects may be actors but that landscape architects are directors, who guide processes to design and affect change." -Jill Desimini, M.L.A. '05

**Shannon Scovell,
701 Studio**

Living Grid Park - MAC
Central Open Space,
ASLA Honor Prize 2008

2007

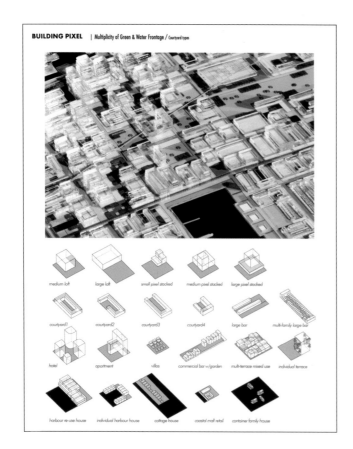

**BUILDING PIXEL** | Multiplicity of Green & Water Frontage / Courtyard types

medium loft    large loft    small pixel stacked    medium pixel stacked    large pixel stacked

courtyard1    courtyard2    courtyard3    courtyard4    large bar    multi-family large bar

hotel    apartment    villas    commercial bar w/garden    multi-terrace mixed use    individual terrace

harbour re-use house    individual harbour house    cottage house    coastal mall retail    container family house

**LARGE SCALE PLAN**

MASSING PIXEL

OPENSPACE PIXEL

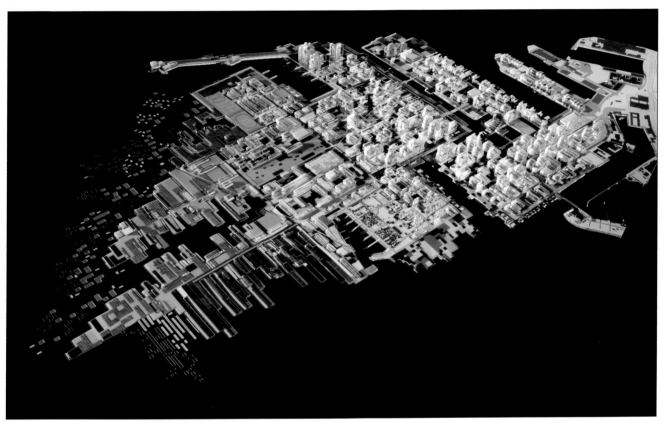

**Youngjoon Choi,
Studio 701**

Living Pixel, completed in
2008, received ArchiPrix
Prize in 2011

**Rebecca Fuchs, Keya Kunte, and Kimberly Cooper, Studio 702**

Seeding Stability: A Strategy for Relocation and Reorganization in a Medellin Barrio, ASLA Honor Prize 2008

Nantawan Sirisup,
Studio 701

2008

In 2009, the first phase of the High Line, designed by James Corner Field Operations, in partnership with architects Diller Scofidio + Renfro and planting designer Piet Oudolf, opened to the public. Once an abandoned rail line, it is now a vibrant elevated park, visited by over 4 million people per year.

Early rendering for
the High Line

"When I was at Penn, I remember sneaking onto the overgrown, undeveloped High Line with my classmates and exploring the urban wilderness." -Heather Ring, M.L.A. '05

**High Line at Night**

2009

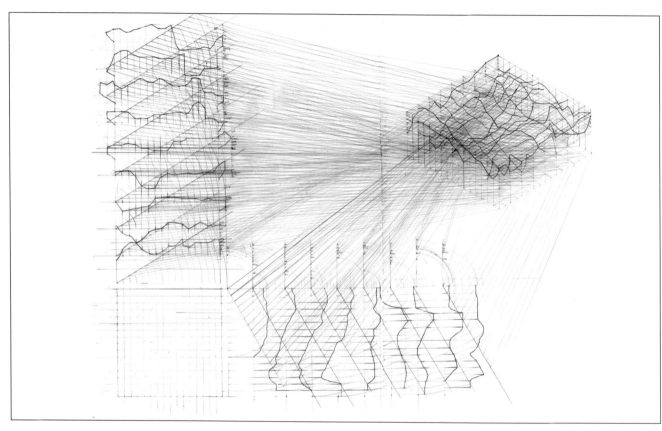

Johanna Barthmaier,
Media I

Emily Vogler, Studio 601

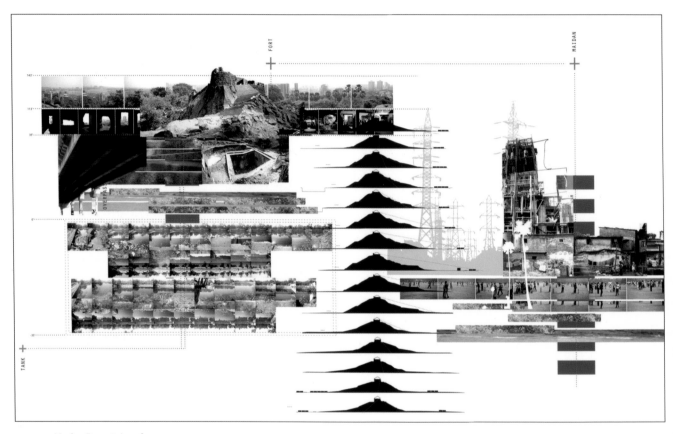

Marisa Bernstein,
Studio 702

Alejandro Vazquez,
Studio 702

2011

185

**Johanna Barthmaier,
Studio 702**

Tempelhof Wasserpark,
ASLA Award of
Excellence 2011

2011

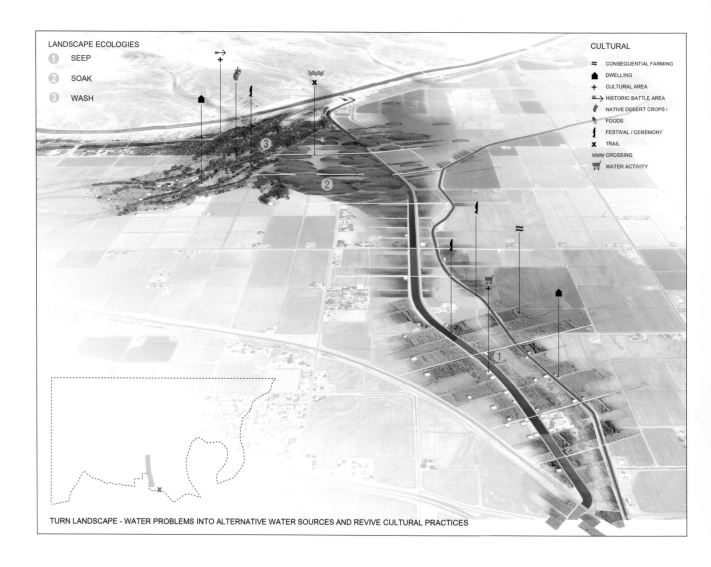

LANDSCAPE ECOLOGIES

1 SEEP
2 SOAK
3 WASH

CULTURAL

≈ CONSEQUENTIAL FARMING
⬟ DWELLING
+ CULTURAL AREA
⤞ HISTORIC BATTLE AREA
🌿 NATIVE DESERT CROPS /
FOODS
🚩 FESTIVAL / CEREMONY
✗ TRAIL
〰 CROSSING
🛒 WATER ACTIVITY

TURN LANDSCAPE - WATER PROBLEMS INTO ALTERNATIVE WATER SOURCES AND REVIVE CULTURAL PRACTICES

# REINTRODUCE DIVERSITY OF TRADITIONALLY CULTIVATED PLANTS

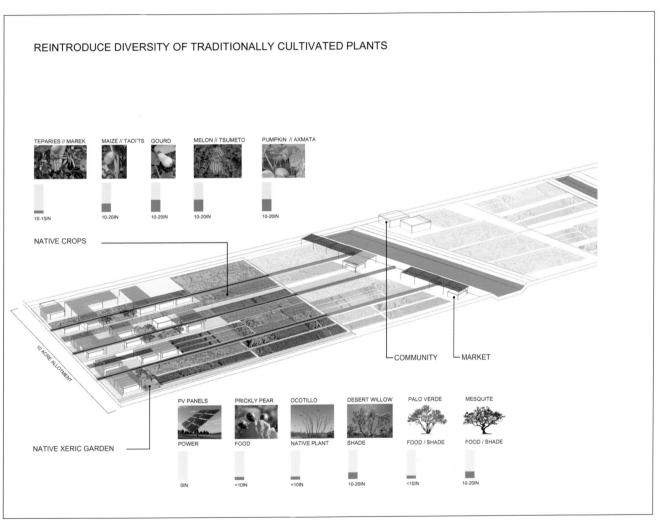

TEPARIES // MAREK    MAIZE // TAOI'TS    GOURD    MELON // TSUMETO    PUMPKIN // AXMATA

10-15IN    10-20IN    10-20IN    10-20IN    10-20IN

NATIVE CROPS

10 ACRE ALLOTMENT

COMMUNITY    MARKET

NATIVE XERIC GARDEN

PV PANELS    PRICKLY PEAR    OCOTILLO    DESERT WILLOW    PALO VERDE    MESQUITE

POWER    FOOD    NATIVE PLANT    SHADE    FOOD / SHADE    FOOD / SHADE

0IN    <10IN    <10IN    10-20IN    <10IN    10-20IN

**Meghan Storm,
Studio 702**

Off the Reservation:
A Seed for Change, ASLA
Honor Award 2012

2012

189

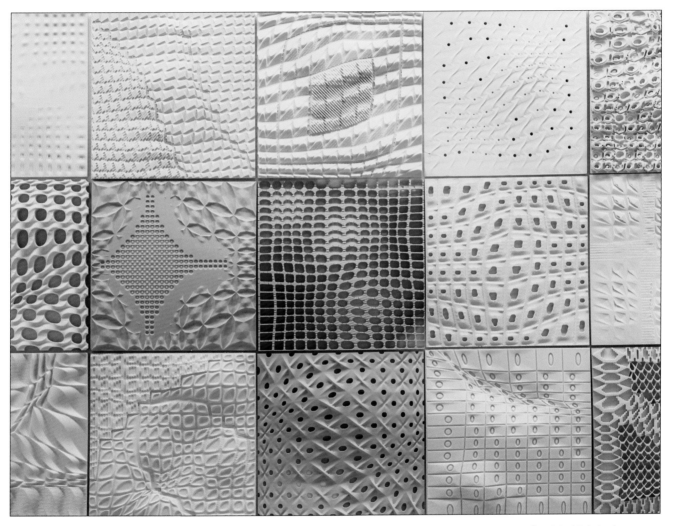

Digital Fabrication,
Final Review

# Richard Weller

# Reflection

In the face of ecological apocalypse one needn't be ashamed of feeling incapacitated, but for landscape architects the situation is more acute because we, unlike any other profession I am aware of, repeatedly say that we are able to do something about it. To wit: in a letter to the New York Times in 1924, Robert Wheelwright, co-founder and co-editor of Landscape Architecture Magazine, a practicing landscape architect and the first director of the program of landscape architecture at Penn, wrote: "There is but one profession whose main objective has been to co-ordinate the works of man with preexistent nature and that is landscape architecture." Devoting his entire career to this very idea, Ian McHarg said it was our imperative to be "stewards of the biosphere—to green the earth, restore the earth [and] heal the earth." In 1984 his successor Anne Whiston Spirn concluded "The Granite Garden" with the edict that the redesign of the city was not just a matter of aesthetics and economics: the very survival of the human race was at stake. And introducing a new compendium of his own writings, James Corner declares that landscape architecture can provide "...the very bedrock, matrix and framework upon which a city can thrive sustainably with nature..."

James Lovelock has said that he would sooner expect a goat to become a gardener than humans to become stewards of the world. But with atmospheric carbon concentration now over 400 parts per million, a global population expected to peak at 10 billion this century and an ecosystem in triage, it would seem we have no choice but to engage in stewardship. Lovelock has also written that what we need are doctors of planetary medicine. McHarg of course provided the diagnosis and the remedy, but the world has proven more complex and chaotic than McHargian planning allowed for. Landscape architects, if they are to make an impact, now need the skills of the planner, the politician and the artist.

In other words, landscape architecture is at best an art of instrumentality and I argue for linking the methods and scales of what we typically differentiate as planning on the one hand and design on the other. In my own work, I have intentionally and selectively worked on projects that range from the detailed semiotics of art in spaces the size of a small room to long-term planning proposals for entire regions. Whilst differences between planning and design have been the source of Penn's intellectual leadership and creativity, the discipline's strength and relevance now lie in their interconnectivity.

In recent decades, landscape architecture has successfully positioned itself as the provider of high quality civic public space, and the recent discourse of landscape urbanism has increased our role in structuring urban design projects, but it cannot be said that we are working successfully at a scale commensurate with the ecological crisis. In line with Penn's legacy, we are now building a research platform specifically to apply design intelligence to landscapes of critical biodiversity which are under pressure from rapid urbanization. While much important scientific work is being done to document the conservation value of 'hotspots', little attention has been applied to specific spatial planning of green infrastructure networks that would help nations meet the United Nation's Convention on Biological Diversity (CBD) targets. In addition to conserving and reconstructing habitat, the CBD emphasizes that these landscapes should be ecologically representative and connected as transnational networks.

Landscape architects should lead the process by which nations can reach the CBD targets. This involves the creative reconciliation of agricultural, industrial, urban development and conservation interests. Not only can this lead to national plans to serve biodiversity, which is in everyone's long-term interest, it can also lead to regional landscape frameworks around which urban growth scenarios can be modeled. As studies by the Yale School of Forestry estimate, there will be approximately another 1.2 million km$^2$ of land subsumed into urban development by 2030 and much of it in the world's biodiversity hotspots.

The Australian paleontologist Tim Flannery and a chorus of others say a massive re-wilding is required so as to restore ecosystem function and "make good the damage of the last 50,000 years." E.O Wilson refers to the protection and restoration of habitat as a "universal moral imperative." McHarg called it stewardship. But the world should come to know it as simply landscape architecture. To achieve this will require the skills of the planner, the politician and the artist.

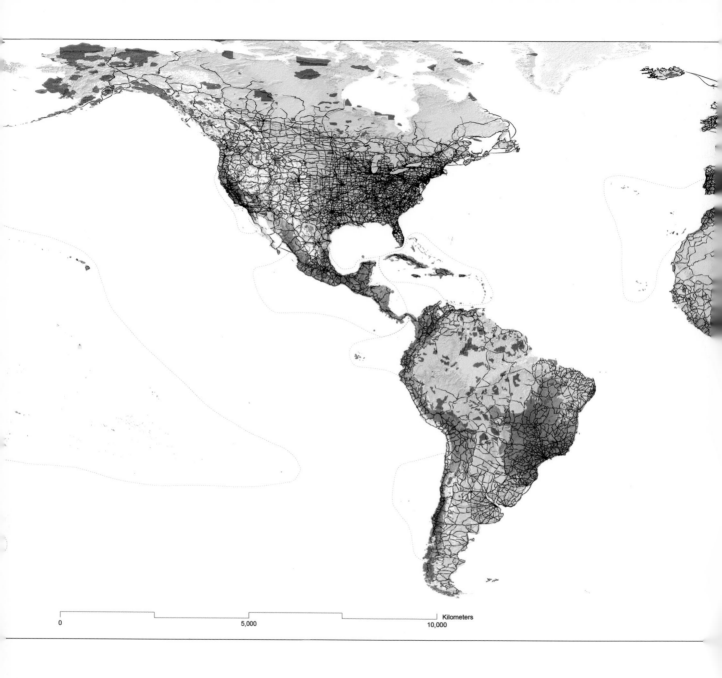

Kilometers

0          5,000          10,000

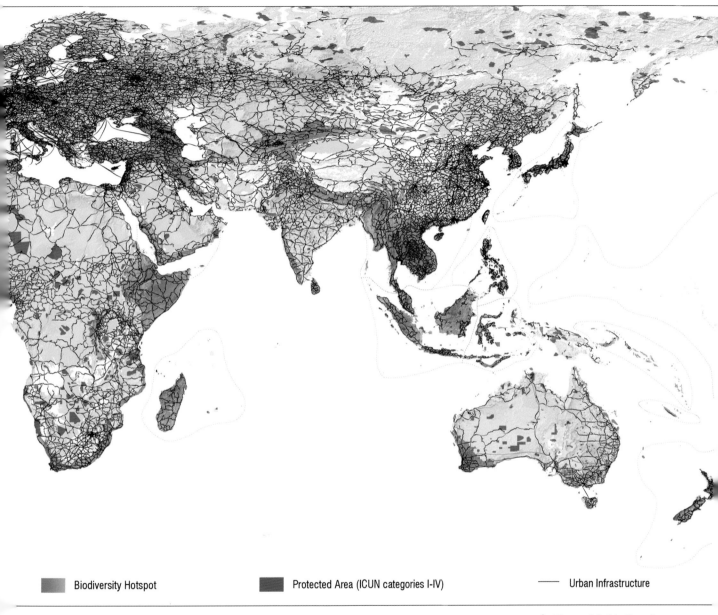

| Biodiversity Hotspot | Protected Area (ICUN categories I-IV) | —— Urban Infrastructure |

**The world's biodiversity hotspots: focal areas for the department's current research program**

Almost 2,200 people have passed through the Landscape Architecture and Regional Planning Department at the School of Design of the University of Pennsylvania.

These are our best efforts to include every professor, lecturer, researcher, administrator and student for the past century. In certain cases, surnames were the only record available.

## 1914–1923

### Lecturers

Burnap, George
Gréber, Jacques

## 1924–1933

### Professors

Schrepfer, Frank
Stevenson, Markley
Wheelwright, Robert

### Students

Ambler, Louis Bartleson
Bailey, Worth Gregory
Baker, James Winsor
Boltz, Clara May
Buell, Courtland F.
Chabanne, Henry Emil
Courter, Jesse Franklin
Cox, Maxine Frances
Davis, Herman Allan
Dewey, Hiram Todd
Edwards, Alfred
Feiss, Carl Lehman
Haines, Katharine W.
Harper, Elizabeth Jane
Henderson, Harold C.
Hornbeck, Agnes Louise neé Russell
Hornbeck, Henry Louis
Hutchings, Horace Lee
Joy, Doris Grace
Julier, Joseph Allen
Laricy, Mercedes C.
Leo, Jean Campbell
Mead, Elizabeth
Mitten, Louise Augusta

Moore, Caroline
Nelson, Gerald Farrington
Nelson, Hubert Swain
Patterson, Frank Engle
Peck, Frederick William
Stuart neé Brown, Edith Crosby
Thompson, Elinor
Tietze, William Robert
Traynor, John Edward
Turrell, Cornelia Howard
Wehrly, Max Siler

## 1934–1943

### Professors

Schrepfer, Frank
Wheelwright, Robert

### Students

Albrecht, Blair Robson
Barnes, Laura
Brand, Oscar Leonard
Bruno, Louis Francis
Bush-Brown, James
Dawson, Jackson
Fanning, Oliver Michael
Farquhar, James
Griffith, John Ramsbottom
Hansen, Harriet Mathilda
Harshberger, Elyonta
Henry, Forrest Richard
Human, Theodore Herbert
Jelinek, Anne
Kemp, Wilfrid Gordon
Kistler, John Seidel
Lamb, James Vincent
Langran, Joe Walter
Levine, Aaron
Lincoln, Henry Allen
May, Henry
Mowry, Helen Perry
Plotkins, Maurice Frank
Reichner, Henry Harold
Saunders, Albert Freeman
Schattner, Marian
Stahl, Annette Manderson
Widenmeyer, Eleanor
Wright, Willard O.

## 1944–1953

### Professors

Baumeister
Borrowicz
Fogg, John
Koyl, George
Langran, Joe
Macguire, John
McCuen
McHarg, Ian

Peck, Frederick
Wild, Carl

### Students

No graduates

## 1954–1963

### Professors, Critics, Researchers

Allison
Andrade
Agle
Baylis, Douglas
Bower
Brown, Michael
Burle Marx, Roberto
Clarke, Lewis
Coornvelt
Cullen, Gordon
Eckbo, Garrett
Enerson, Lawrence
Diamond
Erickson
Fogg, John
Geddes
Glass
Goddard
Godfrey
Gutkind
Halprin, Lawrence
Hansen, Sven
Kiley, Dan
Koyl, George
Koliner, Ralph
Lemco
Li
Linn, Karl
Macguire, John
Mackintosh, Robert
Marzella
McHarg, Ian
Nairn, Ian
Nowicki
Oehme, Wolfgang
Patton, George
Perkins, G. Holmes
Phimister, Donald
Qualls
Roll, Frederick
Romanach
Royston, Robert
Shepheard, Sir Peter
Stevenson, Markley
Schwartz
Scott Brown, Denise
Simon, Jacques
Tatum, George
Van Eyck, Aldo
Venturi, Robert
Vreeland

Walmsley, Anthony
Weissman
Wherry, Dr. Edward
Woodruff

### Students

Arnold, Henry F.
Bartenfeld, Jerry M.
Borrero, Lyda C.
Burggraf, Frank B.
Clemence, Roger D.
Cochrane, Timothy J.
Collens, Geoffrey A.
Dickie, George
Dubin, Lois Sherr
Grant, Benton
Harvey, Robert R.
Hultberg, Erik
Karr, Joseph P.
Kawase, Atsumi
Keene, Joseph P.
Langlay Smith, Gerald M.
Lovinger, Ronald J.
Nicholls, Robert P.
Oliphant, William Jones
Osbaldeston, Roger J.
Phimister, Donald M.
Pinckney, J Edward
Porterfield, Neil H.
Powell, Wendy E.
Rahenkamp, John E.
Rattray, Alexander E.
Reader Jr., Lawrence J.
Rendle, David E.
Roberts, William H.
Sampson, Douglas
Schadt, Richard L.
Shipman, Philip D.
Skelly, Edwin N.
Skinner, David N.
Sloat II, Harry H.
Smart, Charles W W
Tegeder, Gerhard R.
Tyndall, Ian G M
Vroom, Meto J.
Walker, Peter K.
Walmsley, Anthony J.
Waugh, David G H
Whalley, John Mayson
Wilkinson, Denis R.

## 1964–1973

### Professors, Critics, Researchers

Alexander, Robert
Allison
Andrade
Bacon
Borei
Burle Marx, Roberto

Carrothers, Gerald
Cleveland, Francis
Cohen, Dr. Yehudi
Collins, John
Cullen, Gordon
Davidoff
Diamond
DuTot, David
Epstein
Erickson
Faul
Fisher, Dr. Robinson
Fogg, John
Frederickson, David
Frederickson, Vera-Mae
Friedberg, Paul
Friend
George, Dr. John
Geigengack, Dr. Robert
Green
Hanawalt, Dr. Ronald
Hanna, Robert
Hansen, Sven
Hartman, Ronald
Higbee, Dr. Howard
Hyde
Johnson, William
Judson, Dr. Sheldon
Juneja, Narendra
Layman
Levin, Dr. Michael
Li
Linn, Karl
Longenecker, George
Lowry, William
Kane, Thomas
Klein
MacCormack
MacDougall, Dr. E. Bruce
MacIntosh, Robert
Marzella
McCormick, Jack
McHarg, Ian
Meyeroff
Muhlenberg, Dr. Nicholas
Nairn, Ian
Newstein, Dr. Herman
Oehme, Wolfgang
Patrick, Dr. Ruth
Patton, George
Perkins, G. Holmes
Phillips, John
Phimister, Donald
Potts, William
Rahenkamp, John
Reid, Archibald
Reiner
Remson, Dr. Irwin
Richards
Roberts, William

Robinette
Rodenberg
Romanach
Royston, Robert
Rubinoff, Dr. Morris
Schnadelback, Raymond
Scott Brown, Denise
Shagam, Dr. Reginald
Shepheard, Sir Peter
Simon, Jacques
Smith
Snyder, Dr. Robert
Stevens, Benjamin
Strong, Anna Louise
Subitzky, Seymour
Sullivan, Dr. Arthur
Tatum, George
Telfer
Thorsell, Richard
Thoumsim
Throop
Toth, Richard
Tung, Dr. Ted
Van Eyck, Aldo
Venturi, Robert
Vreeland
Wallace
Walmsley, Anthony
Weintraub
Wherry, Dr. Edward
Woodruff
Zandi
Zion, Robert

**Students**

Albert, Frederic G.
Atkins, Jonathan T.
Baker, Terry F.
Beitz, Joseph J.
Belanger, Neal H.
Bensing, Richard T.
Bessey III, Earle D.
Bhan, Ravindra
Bowie, Michael C.
Bradford, Derek
Bradford, Sara Manwell
Butterfield, Griet Terpstra
Caputo, Darryl F.
Carter, Katherine B.
Cheng, Doris Zorensky
Clarke, Michael G.
Cohen, Stuart
Crenshaw, Richard W.
Daher, George A.
Dawson, Marcia Lee
Firth, William R.
Fisher, William R.
Fisk III, Pliny
Flora, Tarsem S.
Folsom, Christopher P.

Franklin, Carol Levy
Franklin, Colin J.
Gisolfi, Peter A.
Glaser, Richard A.
Glotfelty, Caren E.
Grahame, Thomas
Grasso, Anthony M.
Harris, Ruth B.
Hochman, Michael
Hougen, Stewart E.
Howard, William T.
Jefferson, Raymond E.
Jouseau, Marcel R G
Jouseau, Yungkang
Kane, William G.
Khanna, Satish K.
Kihn, Cecily Corcoran
Kinzler, Andrew
Krinsky, Terry A.
Lokhande, Mukund S.
Lyberger, Ronald D.
Maestro, Robert M.
McCloskey Jr., Hewitt B.
McGlade, Dennis C.
Mettee, John M.
Meyer, Darrell C.
Meyers, Charles R.
Morris, Kenneth W.
Moss, Ann W.
Murphy, John E.
Murray, Wesley A.
Nalbandian, Mihran R.
Neff, Susan E Hoag
Neville, Anthony G.
Oman Jr., William M.
Pancoast, John A.
Pattison, Harriet
Ragan, Richard R.
Ramsay, David B.
Rhodeside, Elliot
Rosenberg, William P.
Schraudenbach, Thomas
Sellers III, George Ernest
Shapins, Jerry
Smiley, Michael L.
Stetson IV, John B.
Stich, Alda
Stovall, Allen D.
Streatfield, David C.
Sutliff, Dale A.
Sutphin, Derik F.
Sutton, Jonathan Stone
Talbot, Kenneth W.
Tourbier, H Joachim
Truitt, Peter G.
Turnbull, Wilson Mark
Veltman, James A.
Walton III, Thomas E.
Westmacott, Richard N.
White, Perry J.

Wilson, James R.
Wilson, William L.
Wong, Chi Kui
Young, Alexander

# 1974-1983

**Professors, Critics, Researchers, Administrators**

Ackoff
Allen
Berger, Jonathan
Bockheim, Dr. James
Bott
Cohen, Dr. Yehudi
Collins, John
Cotton
DuTot, David
Edinger
Franklin, Carol
Franklin, Colin
Geigengack, Dr. Robert
Gross, Meir
Halpern
Hamme, David
Hanna, Robert
Harker
James, Frank
Johnson, Dr. Arthur
Juneja, Narendra
Low, Dr. Setha
MacDougall, Dr. E. Bruce
McHarg, Ian
Mills, Robert
Muhlenberg, Dr. Nicholas
Nalbandian, Richard
Olin, Laurie
Patrick, Dr. Ruth
Pierson, Dr. Robert
Putnam, Dr. Stephen
Reifsnyder, Carol
Reiner
Ricklefs
Roberts, William
Rose, Dr. Daniel
Ruby, Dr. Jay
Sagan, Lenore
Sauer, Leslie
Schnadelback, Raymond
Shepheard, Sir Peter
Shore
Siccama, Dr. Thomas
Skaller, Peter
Smith, Dr. Alan
Sprugel, Dr. Douglas
Sullivan, Dr. Arthur
Sullivan, Nathan
Sutton, Jonathan
Tourbier, Dr. Joachim

Vivelo, Frank
Walmsley, Anthony
Wells, Roger
Yeaton, Dr. Richard
Zandi

**Students**

Abbate, Angelo R.
Ahern, John F.
Alminana, Jose M.
Anderson, Katharine D.
Andresen, Anthony M.
Ashenfelter Jr., Richard B.
Aspinwall, William P.
Babus, Steven A.
Badger, Elizabeth A.
Baird, C Timothy
Barringer, Thomas H.
Barton, Eric Chris
Beardslee, Gordon R.
Beck, Michael A.
Berseth, Lynne F.
Bikle, Betsy Wanner
Birdsall, Sarah E.
Biscop, Jean-Luc
Blanco, Sergio J.
Blandford, Christopher J.
Blutstein, Laura J.
Bogner, James E.
Boughton, Jestena C.
Boyar, Henry S.
Boyer, Edward Manuel
Bradley, Charles E.
Brien Jr., Ronald F.
Brink, Lois A.
Brooks, Keith M.
Brooks, Peter R.
Brown, Charles A.
Brown, Cornelia W.
Brown, James R.
Brown, Jay I.
Budd, William W.
Bunster, Ignacio
Calahan Jr., John C.
Cannelos, George J.
Canty, Dennis V.
Chan, Eric P.
Chandavarkar, Nina D.
Chaney, Thomas H.
Chen, Chih Wu
Clark, Veronica Christman
Clarke, Elizabeth Bemis
Collier Jr., Richard C.
Collier, Carol R.
Collins, Donna Jones
Collins, F Arthur
Cook, William A.
Cooney, Carolyn C.
Cooper, Peter B.
Cossaboon, Lewis B.

Coudel, Susan Miller
Cox, Derek W.
Criss, Michael P.
Crone, John V.
Crystal, Roy M.
Curry III, William J.
Dale, Diane M.
Dale, Gerard F.
Daub, David W.
Deis, Jeffrey L.
Della Valle, Elizabeth A.
Deputy, Perseus D.
Deshpande, Dilip Madhav
Diamond, Rusty S.
Diana, Peter A.
Dickerson, Amanda
Dillon, W Reed
Dittmar, Denise M.
Dolan V, Thomas
Donigan, Marie L.
Doolin, James P.
Duffield, Timothy
Duke, Gerallyn D.
Elkinton, Steven
Engel, Gerald A.
Evans, Charles H.
Fairs, Kay
Farley, Alice Hamilton
Farnham, Pamela S.
Fatovic, Robert J.
Fellows, John S.
Ferguson, Bruce K.
Finston, Margaret S.
Fleming III, Robert J.
Fowler Young, L Angela
Froehling, Anne E.
Fuster, Emilio J.
Garfinkel, Donald J.
Garra, Catherine Grissom
Gay, Martha S.
Giampietro, Joseph J.
Goedken, Charlie J.
Goldberg, Paul S.
Goldman, Steven J.
Gray, Brian A.
Griffin, Mary Beck
Groenendaal, Denson L.
Groman, Michael W.
Gulbran Jr., C Edward
Gunderson, Robert J.
Haag Jr., Edgar C.
Haberman, Daniel
Halka, Marie Catherine
Hall, Neil B.
Hansen, Mark W.
Harriss, Martha A.
Hart, Owen L.
Harwell, Faye Brunswic
Harwell, Hugh J.
Hauptmann, Michael G.

Haycock, Patricia M.
Hegemann Clark, Ingeborg E.
Hegemann, David A.
Helm, Andrew H.
Hester, James S.
Hoekenga, Gretchen B.
Hogan, Mary Pat
Hollander, Edmund D.
Huang, Shu Li
Hubler, Stuart A.
Ingram, Kevin J.
James, Anne C.
Jao, Yu Hsing
Jen, Meei-Jane Jane
Jenner, Hadley H.
Jensen, John S.
Jewell, Linda L.
Johnson, Linda M.
Johnson, Robert K.
Judd, Margaret S.
Kalu, Onuoha A.
Kates, David M.
Kates, Katharine Poslosky
Katz, Susan Siegelaub
Kaye, Timothy P.
Keene, Sharon C.
Kellogg, John E.
Kent, Linda
Kester, Kathryn D.
Kettle, James R.
Kim, Jai-Sik
Kim, Sung Woo
Kimmel II, Richard O.
Kingsley, Daniel R.
Kirkland, Stephen T.
Ko, Jewon
Koh, Jusuck
Kolasinski, Sharon L.
Kolb, Brooks R.
Kousky, Laura Friedman
Kowalski, Leon A.
Kressel, Shirley
Kuo, Chyong Y.
Kurokawa, Naoki
Kurz Jr., Frederick N.
Laird, Heidi PAPE
Lamba, Baldev S.
Lampen, Barbara P.
Landry, Antonette
Lane, Michael E.
Lanzetta Jr., Frank J.
Lapins, Andris
Lara Resende, Magda D.
Larsen, Philip W.
Lawrence III, William
Lee, Gary H.
Lehrer, Donna Zarutskie
Leitao, Luiz P.
Leone, Jennifer G.

Lepkowski, Helene
Lerman, Arthur L.
Lewis, C William
Lewis, Robert A.
Librach, Austan S.
Liquori, Lisa M.
Littleton, Peter D.
Loehr, Charles R.
Lucas, Amy
Lundgren, Robert E.
Luzier, John M.
MacKintosh, Amy Rogers
MacLeod, Robert W.
Maechling, Philip L.
Marble, Anne D.
Marini, Robert E.
Marino, Gloria S.
Marshall, Fred S.
Mathews, Katherine I.
Maxwell Jr., Leland P.
McGilvray, Robert D.
McGinty, Gregory F.
McHarg, Carol S.
McIntosh, Alistair T.
McKenzie, Garth
McKenzie, John Stewart
McKenzie, Ricki Levine
Meagher Jr., Donald A.
Meier-Wong, Renie
Melby, Louise Root
Metcalf, Robert B.
Mills, Robert F.
Moore, Russell G.
Mortimer, Albert C.
Motloch, John L.
Moye, Eric M.
Muth, James J.
Nichols, Andrew C.
Nieman, Stephen F.
Nishida, Masanori
Norstog, Jon T.
Norstog, Salisa
Nowicki, Nicole Caupin
Nowicki, Peter L.
O'Byrne, Sara F.
O'Rourke, Peter K.
Oberholzer, Bernard J.
Ogawa, Soichiro
Olcott Jr., John Z.
Ostrauskas, Darius C.
Ostrov, Richard E.
Overton Jr., Edward T.
Owens, Richard Erwin
Parker Jr., James H.
Patrowicz, Scott I.
Patzig, Rodger L.
Pearl, Jacqueline Miller
Pilling II, Joseph Ross
Pillsbury III, Martin K.
Poole III, Samuel E.

Porter, Elizabeth O.
Portnoy, Aron B.
Potter Jr., Robert L.
Price, Helen E.
Prindle, Deborah Z.
Purkess, John E A
Radell, Michael E.
Ratte, Pierre J.
Renner, Cheryl Rosen
Riklin, Joel S.
Rinehart, John F.
Robertson, Iain M.
Robinson, Rodney D.
Rodriguez Fajardo, Trini M.
Roesch, R Geoffrey
Rogers, John W.
Rohrer, William L.
Rose, Jonathan F P
Ross, Valerie R.
Rudoff, Francine G.
Ruff, James C.
Sadler, Samuel R.
Safirstein, Jeffrey M.
Salvatori, Fidenzio G.
Sanchez Flores, Jorge G.
Sanchez, Deborah
Saporta, Elena
Sarrantonio, Ann E.
Satre, Mark S.
Saunders Jr., Ronald M.
Seeley, Richard A.
Seidel, Walter W.
Seltzer, Ethan P.
Seymour, Barbara M.
Sharma, Amar J.
Shrader, Craig C.
Shusterman, Heidi Cooke
Siegel, Ronnie Swire
Smith, Julia Saunier
Smith, Star Louise Flax
Smith, W Gary
Sobotowski, Christopher
Spellmeyer, Bonnie Ellis
Spirn, Anne Whiston
Staniszkis, Jan J.
Stark, Ellen Berman
Stefanakis, Emmanuel
Steiger Olin, Victoria
Steiner, Frederick R.
Stup, Ronald A.
Suarez-Murias, Christine
Syz, Stephan B.
Tang, Paula Leicht
Tanoue, Burt T.
Tetherow, Tim R.
Thayer, Gail Breslow
Thomas, Stephen W.
Toffey, William E.
Tolson, John Paul
Toumayan, Eric G.

Trace, Ronald E.
Turak, Alice
Turner, Robert S.
Unger, Sam S.
Urbanek, Catherine Martin
Van Dyke, Carter
Van Epp, Timothy D.
Vaughan, Deborah
Velsor Jr., Curtis F.
Wall III, Theodore V.
Wallace, Kathleen L.
Walsh, William Joseph
Walter, Richard D.
Walter, Susan Sosik
Watson, Charles R.
Webel, Sandra Lawrance
Weber, Peter A.
Webster, Robert H.
Weiler, Susan K.
Weld Jr., Stephen M.
Wells, Roger
Wenderoth, John H.
Werling, David E.
Weston, Richard
Wheeling, Paul R.
Wiener, Saul S.
Wilkus, Annette P.
Wirtz, Elizabeth L.
Wolfe, Amy Karen
Woodbury, Steven R.
Woods, Susanne
Yoon, Mihae
Zanes III, Roger H.
Zuck, John W.

# 1984-1993

## Professors, Critics, Researchers, Administrators

Alexander, Lee
Anderson, Sally
Andersson, Sven-Ingvar
Arnold, Henry
Baird, Timothy
Beardsley, John
Bemiss, Madge
Browning, Armistead
Bunster, Ignacio
Bye, A. E.
Bye, Edmund
Coe, John
Collins, John
Corner, James
Cramer, Marianne
Creevey, Dr. Lucy
Davis, Francis
Donaghy, Ann
Dowd, Dr. John
DuTot, David

Fein, Albert
Fisk, Pliny
Fleming, Rob
Franklin, Carol
Franklin, Colin
Frey, Susan
George, Dr. John
Giegengack, Dr. Robert
Gleason, Kathryn
Hall, Janice
Halprin, Lawrence
Hamme, David
Hanna, Robert
Heale, Vince
Hollander, Edmund
Janzen, Daniel
Johnson, Dr. Arthur
Johnson, Mark
Judd, Sasi
Keenan, Dr. John
Keene, John
Klein, William
Lager, Anita
Lee, Gary
Low, Dr. Setha
Lowry, William
Major, Judith
McGlade, Dennis
McHarg, Ian
McIntosh, Alistair
McLean, Alex
Miodovnik, Yaki
Muhlenberg, Dr. Nicholas
Murcutt, Glenn
Nairn, MIchael
Napier, Dana
Olin, Laurie
Patrick, Dr. Ruth
Putnam, Dr. Stephen
Radke, John
Robinson, Rodney
Rogers, John
Rose, Dr. Daniel
Ryan, Douglas
Sauer, Leslie
Sauer, Rolf
Schrandenbach, Thomas
Schjetnan, Mario
Shepheard, Sir Peter
Siccama, Dr. Thomas
Sinatra, James
Skaller, Peter
Smith, W. Gary
Snook, Laura
Spirn, Anne Whiston
Stonehill, Dr. David
Sullivan, Nathan
Thorne, Dr. James
Timberlake, James
Tomlin, Dana

Toubier, J, Toby
Tourbier, Joachim
Turbott, Harry
Waldheim, Charles
Walmsley, Anthony
Ward, Allen
Warner, Sam
Wells, Roger
Westcoat, James
Zuchetto, James

## Students

Adewusi, Peter O.
Adhikari, Karen D.
Aganga-Williams, GbolahanEdmund
Agranat, Tarna
Ahmad, Aini
Al-Gilani, Ahmad A.
Al-Harazi, Ahmed G.
Alderson, Jonathan C.
Anderson, Geoffrey L.
Andrews, Lee B.
Astrachan, Zoee
Atkinson, Stephen F.
Atwa, Ali Yahya
Barscz Jr., Charles
Belits, Catherine Ann
Bell, John O.
Berce, Olivera
Berg, John W.
Berger, Alan M.
Bernotas, Christopher J.
Bier, David C.
Biggs, Dawn Renee
Bitsko, Ralph A.
Blackwell-Hafner, Lula
Blackwell, Wendy M.
Boon-Long, Pusdee
Bostwick, Heleigh Ann
Boukenna, Nacima
Boylan II, Francis T.
Brady, Edward D.
Brescia, Elena
Brien, Elizabeth
Britton, Christopher N.
Brose, Lawrence F.
Brownson, Jon A.
Buchan, Alan B.
Bunnag, Pimtawee
Byeon, Wooil
Cacho, Maria
Cameron, Mark S.
Catalano, Lori A.
Chang, Hua-Sun
Chaplick, Joan
Chen, Ching-Fang V.
Chen, Jui-Shu
Chengappa, T M.
Choulika, Tatiana V.

Cohen, Barry R.
Cole, Sherry P.
Cole, Todd R.
Constable, Katharine C.
Corner, James
Crist, Patrick James
Crook, Emery F.
Crusius, Martha Christine
Cserr, Ruth
Cunningham, Sarah T.
Darr, Rebecca E.
David, Steven E.
Davies, Karen S.
Davis, Mathew Jacob
De Jong, Pieter
De Witt, John W.
De, Arijit
Dearhouse, Elisa C.
Deregibus, Katherine
Desai, Bindeeya
Devos-Cole, Suzanne D.
Dickson, Nicholas Rohan
Douglass, Faith Avis
Dugmore, Bruce H.
Dunleavy, Peter
Eck, Robert C.
Eftekhar, Kimberly L.
Eisl, Holger M S
Engle, Reed L.
Evans, Catherine B.
Evans, Elizabeth H.
Every, Daphne S.
Farrell, Julia Moore
Fernandez, Peter R.
Fine, Peter Francis
Folks, Allen K.
Ford, Kathleen A.
Foster, Jeremy A.
Fowler, Theresa Ann
Fuller, Lois H.
Garza, Flora M.
Gest, Kelly L.
Ghezelbash, Reza M.
Girard, Harlan E.
Gless, John T.
Godfrey Jr., Peter
Goldberger, Liliana R. S.
Goldstein, Judith Stern
Gotkin, Michael O.
Gottsegen, Jonathan Mark
Grimm, Harriet Marie
Gross, John M.
Groves, David A.
Hall, Pamella Jean
Hammell, Stephen R.
Han, Youngjun
Hanikian, Karolos
Harris, Amy E.
Hartman III, William C.
Hartman Jr., William R.

Hathaway, Ripley Golovin
Hedlund, Carey Ellen
Helmetag, Peter E.
Hess, Charles E.
Hill, Cynthia M.
Hillebrand, Michael J.
Hornick, Heidi G.
Hostetler, Scott Allan
Hou, Jeffrey
Hoyt, Kimberly A.
Hsu, Wen-Huay
Hu, Lin-Szia
Hu, Tien-Tien S.
Hurley-Kurtz, Pauline
Hwang, Lan-Shing
Ingoldsby, Joseph E.
Ishak, Benjamin
Ishak, Dani M.
Ishii, Akiko
Johnson, Virginia L.
Jones, Cat E.
Kagel, Nancy Liebrecht
Kang, Euisouk
Kang, Fang-Ming
Karasik, Myra
Karlsson Jr., Carl E.
Karlsson, Lucy C.
Kelley, Mary Jaron
Kent, Nancy Balderston
Kim, Seung-Tae
Kim, Sung-Kyun
Kim, Yoon Ha
Kingslow, Marcia E.
Kirkwood, Niall Gordon
Koch, Steven E.
Konieczny, Mary W.
Koreman, Elizabeth
Korostoff, Neil Philip
Lamb, David R.
Lange, David A.
Leder-Pack, Beth Ann
Lee, Jennifer Storrs
Lee, Sondra D.
Lee, Tae-Woong W.
Lee, Yong-Woo
Leisner, Richard Kent
Lemmerman, Patricia
Lepard Jr., Paul E.
Lewis, Benjamin G.
Li, Yu-Chich
Limpaiboon, Apinya
Lin, Chiiruey
Lin, Chun-Hsu
Lin, Dah Yuan
Lin, Ko-Yu
Lin, Wen-Yen
Littleton, Joanna Margaret
Loewe, Ruth Shaw
Longsworth, Gordon H.
Lukens, Elizabeth Brockie

MacFarlane, Christopher
Maddock, Rupert B.
Marano, Mary A.
Marchal, Patrice
Marcucci, Daniel J.
Mat, Noriah
Mathur, Anuradha
McCoubrey, Stephen M.
Messer, Elizabeth
Michaux, Jon C.
Miller, R Matthew
Minich, Nancy A.
Miodovnik, Jacov Y.
Misslbeck, Heidi Gene
Mohamed, Noorizan
Morrissey, Michael Todd
Munawar, Rizal
Murphy, Donna Marie
Nairn, Michael P.
Newton, Richard A.
Ng, Bernard
O'Brien, Regina
O'Donnell, Nancy Q.
Oates, G Anthony
Ogle, Kim R.
Olgyay, Cora L.
Ostrich, David Joseph
Pal, Aditya Kumar
Patel, Maneesha A.
Patel, Nanda S.
Peerson, Susan R.
Penny-Lautrup, Elizabeth
Pete, Richard H.
Pierce, Devon Carlin
Pierce, Robert James
Pollio, Michele S.
Poor, Jeffrey S.
Porter, Sarah Hughes
Poulter, Simon Anthony
Pressman, Michael
Principato, Sharon F.
Pugliese, Christopher L.
Quigley, Patricia A.
Raphael, Ruth A.
Real De Asua, Rafael
Redway, Mary T.
Regnier, Julie E.
Reutlinger, Karen A.
Rhees, Suzanne Sutro
Richardson, Alice Elmore
Riddell, Bruce John
Rikhoff, Jeffrey Jon
Risna, I Wayan
Rodriguez Trigo, Maria J.
Rookwood, Paul M.
Rosenzweig, Laura
Rube, Paul J.
Ryan, Christopher M.
Saari, Kurt D.
Samuel, Peter Bernhardt

Sanders, Lucinda R.
Sasaki, Takeshi
Scandura, Jeanne M.
Schneider, John Eric
Schulman, David M.
Schulman, Samuel
Seppi, Joseph R.
Shang, Hwa-Yuan
Sharp, Elissa MacKenzie
Shaulson, Beth Arnold
Sherif, Aubrey N.
Sheu, Dah Win
Shim, Woo Chang
Shuster, Forrest W H
Shymanski, Gregory P.
Skehan, D. Conor
Soghor, Lisa Valerie
Soin, Devinder Singh
Son, Sunok
Starr, Laura
Steppacher, Brian
Stigberg, Robert Gunnar
Stoddard, Carolynn Ruth
Sukotjo, Lilia Setiprawart
Sun, Shu-Ling
Sun, Yige
Sykes, J Andrew
Tariq, Mohammad
Teng, Wan-Jiun
Terranova, Jill Marie
Tesler, Charles Robert
Theurkauf, Edward August
Thompson, Ana D.
Thompson, Bradley
Tochikura, Kyo
Tolba, Osama
Trevathan, Sandy J.
Tsai, Te-I Albert
Tsaoussis, Milia
Vissilia, Anna-Maria
Wahl, Tamela Jean
Wall, Gerard Michael
Wallenmeyer, Phyllis
Wang, Hweywen
Wang, Pi-Fen
Warren, Barbara Carnes
Way, Shirley D.
Webb, Scott Thomas
Weng, Hsiung-Lun
Wheat, Sherry
Whipple, Scott Wesley
Wilks, Barbara Ellyn
Williams, J Howard
Williams, Stacie Jean
Wilson, John Frederick
Wiriadinata, Arief
Wisselmann-Gold, Julia
Wolfe, Elizabeth Ellen
Wood, Barbara Eileen
Wood, Jeffrey R.

Xu, Ping
Xu, Wei
Yap, James S.
Ye, Xue
Yee, Carl J.
Yontar, Neyran
Yoshimi, Rumi
Zaki, Mohamed S.
Zeevy, Shlomo
Zehnder, Matthew I.
Zelzman, Patricia L.
Zhai, Jun
Zlocki, Christopher J.

# 1994-2003

**Professors, Critics, Researchers, Administrators**

Abrioux, Yves
Acconci, Vito
Ali, Zakiyyah
Allen, Stan
Anderson, Geoffrey
Arnaiz, Carlos Ramon
Bargmann, Julie
Beardsley, John
Beaumont, Rodney
Bedell, Robert
Benn-Aissa, Ramla
Berman, R
Bemiss, Margaret
Berque, Augustin
Berrizbeitia, Anita
Blank, Alice
Bott, Thomas
Bunster-Ossa, Ignacio
Bürgi, Paolo
Burratoni, Gianni
Bye, Arthur
Casper, Brenda
Cavallero, Alberto
Cheetham, Robert
Connelly, Peter
Cook, Robert
Cooperman, Emily
Corner, James
Cosgrove, Denis
Cywinski, Bernard
Czerniak, Julie
da Cunha, Dilip
Davis, Matthew
Descombes, George
Desvigne, Michel
Donaghy, Ann
Douglas, Kim
DuTot, David
Evans, Shawn
Faga, Barbara
Falck, Lindsay

Forrester, Anna
Foster, Dr. Jeremy
Franklin, Carol
Fung, Stanislaus
Galletti, Georgio
Gastil, Raymond
Gilbert, Cristen
Gillette, Jane
Gleason, Kathryn
Gouverneur, David
Griswold, Mac
Groening, Gert
Hall, David
Halprin, Lawrence
Hanna, Robert
Hara, Mami
Harkavy, Ira
Harvey, David
Harwell, Faye
Hauxner, Marlene
Hays, David
Heintz, Judith
Henderson, Ron
Hoffman, Denise
Holtzapple, Laurel
Hood, Walter
Horn, Claudia
Horvath, Jamie
Hoxie, Chris
Hunt, John DIxon
Janosky, Karen
Jeong, Wookju
John-Adler, Kate
Johnson, Arthur
Kahn, Andrea
Keeney, Gavin
Keller, Ed
Kelley, Daniel
Khan, Nancy
Kim, Katherine
King, Bobbie
Kirkwood, Niall
Klein, James
Kollar, Jennifer
Krog, Steven
Kulper, Perry
Kunze, Donald
Lager, Anita
Lardner, Elizabeth
Lassus, Bernard
Latz, Peter
Lee, Brian
Low, Dr. Setha
Ludwig, James
Lutz, Winifred
MacLean, Alex
Mardeusz, Stuart
Marot, Sebastien
Marpillero, Sandra
Marshall, Victoria

Marton, Deborah
Mathur, Anuradha
Maurer, Joseph
McFarlan, Jan
McGlade, Dennis
McGloughlin, Charles
McHarg, Ian
McIntosh, Allistair
McPeters, Keith
McSherry, Laurel
Merchant, Carolyn
Meyer, Elizabeth
Meyer, Paul
Miller, Lynden
Miodovnik, Yaki
Miss, Mary
Moody, Sarah
Moore, Andrew
Mosbach, Catherine
Murcutt, Glenn
Neer, Charles
Napier, Dana
Napper, Deborah
Naranjos, Carlos
Neises, Ellen
Newton, Richard
Nielson, Signe
Oehme, Wolfgang
Olgyay, Cora
Olin, Laurie
O'Malley, Therese
O'Shea, Peter
Palms, Sylvia
Parrett, Julie
Perez de Vega, Eva
Pinto, Jody
Playdon, Dennis
Pollak, Linda
Pringle, Diane
Quennell, Nicholas
Raabe, Peta
Reed, Christopher
Reiser, Jesse
Reo, Jonathan
Rhoads, Ann
Ridgway, Christopher
Robertson, Dr. David
Robinson, Rodney
Rookwood, Paul
Rose, Dr. Dan
Ross, Andrew
Rubin, David
Ruddick, Margie
Ruy, David
Sanders, Lucinda
Sauer, Leslie
Scholz-Barth, Katrin
Schuldenfrei, Eric
Schwartz, Martha
Scott Brown, Denise

Shepheard, Paul
Shepheard, Sir Peter
Shorban, Ekaterina
Shvidkovsky, Dmitry
Silberberg, Ramsey
Smith, W. Gary
Smith, Ken
Spens, Michael
Spirn, Anne Whiston
Stilgoe, John
Thorne, James
Tomlin, Dr. Dana
Treseder, Kathleen
Tupu, Steven
Umemoto, Nanako
Urban, James
Urbanski, Matthew
Vaughan, Terry
Waldheim, Charles
Walker, Paul
Walker, Peter
Wall, Alex
Wedlick, Dennis
Weiss, Allen
Wescoat, James
Wibiralske, Anne
Willig, Dr. Sarah
Wines, James
Wu, Mei
Zlocki, Christopher

**Students**

Aibel, Laura M.
Al-Gilani, Abdulkader A.
Anazawa, Junko
Apte, Suvarna
Arab, Michelle
Arnold, Lisa R.
Asawa, Elizabeth E.
Baratta, Eric A.
Barbieri, Craig A C
Bardorf, Stephen P.
Bartenhagen, Jessica W.
Bell, Julia
Bhat, Prashant N.
Blair, Clarissa F.
Bonanni, Lori
Booth, Eliza
Brondo, Edmundo U.
Burkett, Catherine M.
Cahill, Deborah A.
Capiaux, Corinne E.
Capone, Veronna B.
Carle, Diane Stella
Carlson, David B.
Carter, Pei-Chih Kao
Cash, Brooke Whiting
Cass, Lisa
Chan, Vella
Chang, Chen-Chen

Chang, Shyh-Yueh
Cheetham, Robert M.
Chen, Chia-Chun
Chen, Keng-Chun
Chen, Shih-Ying
Cheon, Jae-Hyun
Chiang, Meng-Yuan
Chien, Hui-Cheng
Cho, Eun Young
Cho, Yoon Chul
Chon, Jin-Hyung
Chu, Shih-Jen
Chuang, Cheng-Ying
Chuang, Shih-Ying
Chung, Alice Shin-Ying
Chung, Keunwoo
Clark, Lundy
Claytor, Warren Ingersoll
Cohen, Tracey
Coignet, Philippe
Cooney, Amy V.
Cordero, Vanessa
Crowley, Michelle Hollins
Cullen, Jennifer E.
Culp, Carrie J.
Curran, Charles C.
Daly, Dorothy Ann
Davis, Joanne Tamar
Davison, Mark
Davivongs, Vudipong
Delcambre, Carla
Denk, Danielle M.
DeVuono, Julia Wood
Diez, Felipe
Dinep, Claudia
Doherty, Gareth G.
Douglas, Kimberlee Joyce
Duncan, Alison C.
Eleey, Patrick Luke
Engelking Wright, Bianca
Giannetto, Raffaella
Falcone, Anthony L.
Fein, Thomas E.
Fisfis, Persefoni J.
Forrester, Anna
Frantz, Matthew Thomas
Freitag, Amy L.
Fukuoka, Takanori
Garcia-Anguiano, Federico
Gardocki, Mary L.
Garland, Hyojung Kim
Garrigan, Sean C.
Gharaibeh, Anne
Gill, Kamni
Gonzalez Juaristi, Alejandro
Gottscho, Jonathan A.
Greenspan, Adam
Guillette, Anne K.
Guldalian, Eric L.
Hallmark, Andrea E.

Hamill, Elizabeth C.
Hanano, Miwako
Harnish, Anne E.
Harper, David R.
Harris, Albert E.
Hashimoto, Masahiko
Hatae, Hiroshi
Hau, Peter
Hedao, Prashant M.
Henderson, Ronald E.
Hetzel, Erik W.
Hickin, Christopher
Hofmann, Tyrone G.
Holland, Sarah A.
Horn, Claudia Meyer
Horst, Jenifer E.
Hsu, Yih-Ming
Huang, Shih-Fang
Huang, Yi-Yu
Humphreys, Laurie F.
Hur, Kyu
Husta, Eric Anthony
Iitomi, Mika
Ishida, Naoto
Iyer, Swarna Lata
Jacobs, Shira
Jeong, Wookju
Kainer, Rebecca E.
Karwacki, Andrzej
Keltai, Kenneth A.
Kim, Chung Hwan
Kim, Hyun-Jung
Kim, Soon-Boon
Kim, Sujin
Knox, Martin Jeffrey
Kuchinsky, Benjamin S.
LaDuca, John J.
Lanstra- Nothdurft,Ardith
Lee, Brian D.
Lee, Byoung-Eun
Lee, Hui-Li
Lee, Yumi
Leelapattanaputi, Veera
Lenihan, Caitlin Jean
Lewis, Thomas Schouten
Liang, Shu-Hua
Liao, Kuei-Hsien
Liao, Shian-Po
Liao, Te-Hsuan
Lin, Meng-Li
Lin, Yu-Wen
Ling, Chih-Chiun
Ling, Stella F.
Loeb, Deenah E.
Long, Seen Hui
Lu, Shiau-Yun
Luangsuwan, Worasak
Lundeen, Patricia Ann
Luo, Ye
Lussier, Carolyn J.

Mahanger, Deborah
Marshall, Victoria Jane
Martin, Christina C.
Masucci, Katharine Martin
Matson, William J.
Maurer, Joseph
Mccrea, Todd Byron
Miles, Lisa H.
Moon, Cary C.
Morse, Martin H.
Moscony, Stephen T.
Motonaga, Mark Kenji
Mullahy, James
Mustafa, Maged
Nagel, Catherine Jane
Nakamuta, Tadaaki
Neer, Charles Bruce
Neises, Ellen
Okada, Kaori
Ono, Akiko
Palms, Sylvia
Parrett, Julie
Pei, Kuang-Tu
Perona-Falcone, Severn M.
Pohl, John W.
Prendiville, Patricia A.
Pritchard, Leslie Suzanne
Querry Jr., James
Razi, Marisa Leila
Reed, Christopher S.
Richard, Bryn L.
Rockwell, Heather M.
Roth, Gary Antal
Ryan, Richard L.
Ryu, Wonsang
Salazar-Jasbon, Alejandro
Salzer, Erin P.
Sattler, Steven M.
Schuh, Sara Pevaroff
Sharon, John Thomas
Shen, Tung-Sheng
Shen, William
Sherrod, Alice Hovater
Shon, Bang
Siciliano, Paul
Silberberg, Ramsey E.
Simmchen, Carina
Sitisara, Naphatsakorn
Snell, Julie A.
Son, Ji In
Spokus, Kelly A.
Spulecki, E Allan
Staudt, Robert C.
Steen, Jill
Sterling-Boyers, Rachel
Stewart, Alexander
Sukolratanametee, Sineenart
Suriyachan, Chamawong
Switala, Kevin J.

Switkin, Lisa
Szura, Michael
Tamir, Karen
Tang, Chia-Wei
Tantinipankul, Worrasit
Tessier III, Donald E
Thomann, Mark B.
Thompson, Jeanne J.
Tominaga, Mariko
Torres, Rene L C
Trefny, Gretchen
Truesdale, Elizabeth H.
Tsai, Ming-Hsiu
Tsai, Yi-Chun
Tsuboi, Yuta
Tsurusaki, Tsuneo
Tsurushima, Koichi
Tsuruta Cramer, Keiko
Tung, Tsung-Ming
Tutora, Marcia L.
Uribe, Patricia
Whealan, Carolyn
Wiley, Catherine Ann
Wu, Chien-Hui
Wu, Lei
Wu, Mei
Yamamoto, Tetsuya
Yang, Chia-Wen
Yoshida, Kenichi
Young, Steven J.
Zhou, Hong
Zmudzka, Anna

# 2004-2013

## Professors, Critics, Researchers, Administrators

Appelhans, Kira
Arnaiz, Carlos
Austin, Jason
Bainbridge, Sierra
Beamer, Tiffany
Beckman, Julie
Benedito, Silvia
Berger, Elke
Berrizbeitia, Anita
Boyce, Hallie
Brown, Jessica
Bürgi, Paolo
Burke, Megan
Burrell, Greg
Cadaval, Eduardo
Chhiba, Kiran
Cook, Neil
Corner, James
da Cunha, Dilip
Disponzio, Joseph
Falck, Lindsay
Franklin, Carol

Franklin, Colin
Freese, Joshua
Garcia, Steven
Gelles, Richie
Giannetto, Raffaella Fabiani
Gouverneur, David
Gross, Ron
Hart, Marie
Heavers, Nathan
Henson, Jessica
Hopkins, John
Jeong, Wookju
John-Adler, Kate
Johnston, Rachel
Kainer, Rebecca
Kao, Stephanie
Kaseman, Keith
Keller, Ed
Kennedy, Richard
Kollar, Jennifer
Latz, Peter
Lee, Trevor
Lenneiye, Thabo
Lucia, Andrew,
Lutsky, Karen
Maestres, David
Marcinkowski, Christopher
Marpillero, Sandro
Marshall, Victoria
Martic, Danilo
Martin, Katherine
Mathur, Anuradha
Maurer, Joseph
McFarlan, Jan
M'Closkey, Karen
McGlade, Dennis
Meehan, Douglas
Meyer, Paul
Miller, Michael
Minson, Eve
Moin, Sahar
Montgomery, Todd
Morabito, Valerio
Mosbach, Catherine
Neises, Ellen
Olgyay, Cora
Olin, Laurie
Orr, Jennifer
Ostrich, David
Pevzner, Nicholas
Pollak, Linda
Pringle, Diane
Reed, Chris
Rein-Cano, Martin
Rivera-Diaz, Yadiel
Robertson, David
Robinson, Rodney
Ruddick, Margie
Ruy, David
Ryan, Tom

Salem, Leigh
Sanders, Lucinda
Scholz-Barth, Katrin
Schuldenfrei,
Sen, Sanjukta
Solor, Cristen
Sowell, Jason
Switkin, Lisa
Tabet, Abdallah
Taborda, Claudia
Tamir, Karen
Thomann, Mark
Tomlin, Dana
Toy, Jennifer
Tupu, Steven
Umemoto, Nanako
Van Buskirk, Darcy
VanDerSys, Keith
Van Eyck, Jerry
Weidner Astheimer, Sarah
Weiler, Susan
Weiler, Richard
Willig, Sarah
Witte, David
Wu, Mei
Wunsch, Aaron
Young, William
Zhou, Hong

## Students

Addington, Jason
Agriodimas, Irene
Ahern, Rachel M.
Ahn, Donghyouk
Allard, Francisco
Almodovar, Stefanie I.
Anderson, Jane E.
Appelhans, Kira
Arrendondo, Jorge
Asai, Miki
Ashworth Jr., Daniel Allen
Austin, Jason Timberlake
Austin, Roydrick T
Bae, Jungyoon
Bahadorzadeh, Yasamin
Ball, Jessica L.
Barensfeld, Mary Evans
Bennett, James M.
Bermudez, Diego
Bernstein, Marisa S.
Bessho, Tsutomu
Betnar, Bret O.
Beyer, Lisa M.
Bishop, Scott Foster
Bleakley, Christopher R.
Boland, Rana J.
Booher, Aaron
Born, Megan M.
Bosse, Alexa R.
Braga, Caroline L.

Braquet, Ashley M
Brown, Jessica H
Burgess,Taylor S.
Burgi, Stephan L.
Burke, Megan M.
Burrows, Susanna B.
Cai, Jing
Canter, Julie D.
Cao, Ningxiao
Carey, Laura G.
Carter, Leslie J.
Casariego, Jonay
Casillas, Jean Pierre
Castilla, Isabel
Castro, Samantha Lynne
Cella, Kathleen C.
Cha, Minhi
Chang, Ho Ling
Chang, Po-Shan
Chawla, Purva
Chen, Chia-Chi
Chen, Hsinyi Misa
Chen, Kuan-Chang
Chen, Rong
Chen, Wei
Chen, Yongjia
Chen, Zhe
Cheng, Hang
Chiang, Jung-En
Chiarelli, Elizabeth L.
Chiu, Chen-Yin
Chiu, Roman
Chiu, Yu-Han
Cho, Koung Jin
Choi, Bun Gyu
Choi, Hye Young
Choi, Jisu
Choi, Minyoung
Choi, Youngjoon
Chou, Shu-Hsien
Choy, Amy W.
Chung, Christopher S.
Ciammaichella, Lily Trinh
Clark, Anne
Clifford, Martha J.
Cohen, Aron G.
Collier, Elizabeth F.
Confair Jr., Edward D.
Cooper, Kimberly A.
Cortinas, Adrian
Cui, Muhan
Current, Jennifer A.
Czulak, Victor
Dai, Yang
Daniels, Jennifer Lynn
Davies, Kimberly L.
Davis, Adam Goodfellow
Davis, Hannah
Dawson, Andrew G.
Day, Frederick

Degregorio, Michael A.
Desbiens, Martha Suzanne
Desimini, Jill Elizabeth
Dickman, Nathan P.
Diptee, Wess
Doherty, Barrett H.
Dong, Yajun
Dougherty, Julia Ann
Dougherty, Megan
Duan, Shanshan
Duxbury, David C.
Dwyre, Cathryn M.
Ells, Matthew P.
Fan, Zhuangyuan
Fang, Chenlu
Farquhar, Kathryn H.
Fehrmann, Adrian
Fein, Jessica S.
Felder, Nyasha
Fellman, Claire L.
Finan, Brooke Marie
Fisher, Richard
Foster, David C.
Foy, Robert M
Frank, Ilse L.
Fristensky, Jason P
Fuchs, Rebecca M.
Gabrielian, Aroussiak
Gao, Kuan
Gardner, Colin
Gates, Sally G.
Goetz, Michael B.
Graziano, Christine
Gruberg, Diana N
Grunfeld, Miriam
Gupta, Ekta
Hallett, Sarah Jane
Han, Sa Min
Han, Xiaoye
Hanby, Peter B.
Hansen, Andrea L.
Hart, Marie F.
Harvey, Katherine C.
Hauck, Lauren
Haynes, Susan
Heavers, Nathan M.
Hein, Jonathan
Henry, Kordae
Henry, Tamara M.
Henson, Jessica M.
Heo, Biyoung
Hernandez Fontanez,
Annabelle
Herpmann, Brenna C.
Higgins, Caitrin S.
Hirsch, Alison B.
Hoch, Claire L
Hower, James F.
Hsu, Huai-Jen

Hsu, Jui-Sheng
Hu, Vivian Y.
Hu, Yishuo
Hua, Lin
Huang, Chieh
Huang, Kerry W.
Huang, Yujia
Hunt, Julia
Jacobs, Michael L.
Jain, Anjali
Jankowsky, Margaret L.
Jarrett, Matthew Edward
Jee, Rebecca A.
Jencks, Lily C.
Jensvold, Taran
Jeon, Eunhye
Jie, Xiaohan
Jo, Yong Jun
Johnson, Janelle L.
Johnson, Laura Marie
Johnson, Robert
Johnston, Rachel Ann
Jones, Angelina
Jones, Jeffrey
Juang, Huei Ming
Jung, Hyun-Bum
Junkin, Christopher
Kaiser, Michaela Kathleen
Kang, Leeju
Kao, Pei-Ching
Kaplan, Taylor A.
Karaman, Joanna
Kato, Naoko
Kaufer, Anneliza Carmalt
Ke, Dan
Keary, Elizabeth
Kelly, Elizabeth Campbell
Kern, Keyleigh N.
Kessler, Brett
Ki, Hyosoon
Kieser, Mark J
Kim, Eunjee
Kim, Harry
Kim, Hyun Suk
Kim, Hyun-Min
Kim, Miseon
Kim, Sung Hun
Kim, Sung Joon
Kim, Youngsoo
King, Emily
Koff, Nicolas
Kominsky, Jamee R.
Kuang, Huiqing
Kubik, Joseph A.
Kwon, Min-Suk
Kwon, Yu
Ladjevardi, Agnes
Lan, Shih-Lin
Lau, Gloria K.
Leahy, Shannon W.

Lederer, Rebecca R.
Lee, Chi-Yin
Lee, Ho Young
Lee, Janet H.
Lee, Jeong Hwa
Lee, Jiae
Lee, Jinwook
Lee, Kyung Keun
Lee, Sanghoon
Lehrman, Barry Joel
Levin, Melissa B.
Levy, Noah Z.
Li, Wen
Li, Xi
Li, Xun
Li, Yi
Li, Yiran
Li, Zhongwei
Liang, Hao
Lim, Sanghyun
Lin, Connie P.
Lin, Michelle
Lin, Yu-Ju
Lindquist, Michael G.
Linsenmayer, Amy A.
Liu, Linyu
Liu, Sheng
Liu, Tianyang
Liu,Xi
Liu, YIng
Loomis, Stefanie M
Loui, Kristi A.
Lu, Wenwen
Ludwig, Ashley B.
Luo, Yadan
Lutsky, Karen O.
Maccuaig, Lauren M.
MacDonald, Thomas
Mahoney, Suzanne
Mandel, Lauren N.
Mannion, Rosalynn A.
Mao, Wei
Martic, Danilo I.
Martin, Katherine L.
Martinez, Jacqueline
Marwil, Joseph I.
Mccabe, Erin A
McConnico, Stephen A.
Mcinerny, Austin F.
McLeod, Robert J.
Mcmillan, Melinda
McVeigh, Brian
Meehan, Douglas J.
Michael, David Kenneth
Miller, Michael W.
Min, Katy Hyunjoo
Miyahara, Katsunori
Mizan, Shushmita B
Moin, Sahar
Molter, Karli A.

Montgomery, Todd H.
Mui, Jennifer Dik-Young
Murata, Misako
Nam, Hyunjoo
Nam, Ji Young
Nameth, Jillian B.
Neye, Emily B.
Nicolosi-Endo, Benjamin
O'Connor, Kyle D.
O'Meara, Kathleen M.
Oat-Judge, Hilary A.
Ohly, John H.
Olson, Alyssa K.
Ombregt, Wouter
Orr, Jennifer Lynn
Pan, Yirui
Park, Adela
Park, Anna
Park, Chiyoung
Park, Soohyun A.
Park, Su-Jung
Patel, Anoop V.
Patterson, Kaarin L.
Peck, Sarah K.
Pevzner, Nicholas
Phelps, Johanna O.
Phillips, James
Pierce-Delaney, Meaghan
Pirie, Andrew C.
Policarpio, Mark
Popowsky, Rebecca S.
Poupeau, Francois
Prentice, Graham L.
Privitera, Paul
Qi, Fan
Qi, Yi
Rabiee, Zeinab
Ragulina, Svetlana
Rahim, Anooshey
Reber, Annabelle Gibson
Reynolds, Sally A.
Ring, Heather
Ritchie, Megan Denise
Rivera-Diaz, Yadiel J.
Roberts, Rachel A.
Robleto Costante,
Leonardo E
Rockcastle, Maura
Rodgers, Katherine
Rosenburg, Joseph
Rossi-Mastracci, Jessica L.
Rothery, Misako
Rouhi, Alaleh
Rousse, Pierre
Rovzar, Mariana
Rubenstein, Heather Kaye
Rubenstein, Patricia Anne
Rukkulchon, Pattarapan
Rule, Lindsay
Saenz, Daniel

Sandorff, Ingrid V W
Santamaria Ruval, Eduardo
Schatz, Adam K.
Schlatter, Andrew M.
Schneider, Ann M.
Schue, Allison K.
Schundler, Brian F.
Scott, Emily M.
Scovell, Shannon Victoria
Seek, Amy
Seiter, David Gordon
Sen, Sanjukta
Seyfried, Joshua B
Shafir, Michael
Shahid, Amirah A.
Shi, Huilai
Shi, Xiayao
Shih, Yi-Chu
Shim, Bo Won
Shin, Da Young
Shin, Sookyung
Siek, Leslie Russell White
Silber, Emily
Sinclair, Ian M
Sirisup, Nantawan
Skepnek, Riggs P.
Smith, Abigail H.
Smith, Michael W
Solovieva, Maria A.
Song, Byung Eon
Song, Ting
Soong, Angela C.
Soule, Matthew G.
Sparks, Gregory B.
Squier-Roper, Caitlin M.
Stetson, Elizabeth T.
Storm, Meghan T.
Stromberg, Timothy
Studer, Megan C.
Su, Hang
Su, Shunkuang
Suganuma, Yuka
Sun, Difeng
Swanson, Lewis T.
Sweeting, Naima A
Tabet, Abdallah S.
Talarowski, Meghan R.
Tan, Chun Yan Katie
Tang, Kenneth W.
Tang, Qiuhong
Taylor, Emerson Angell
Templeton, Caroline Dix
Tenyenhuis, James
Tian, Siyu
Tomura, Eiko
Tsai, Miao-Chi
Tsay, Meng-Lin
Tsutsumi, Yuichiro
Tucker, Steven M.

Ulrich, Stephanie M.
Valk, Eliza S.
Van Geldern, Emily
Vanno, Sirintra
Vazquez, Alejandro D.
Venonsky, Judy E.
Viquez, Dana L.
Visconti, Autumn
Wang, Guangping
Wang, Haoyang
Wang, Jiaqi
Wang, Jing
Wang, Tengteng
Wang, Yi
Wang, Yifan
Wang, Yitian
Wang, Ziwei
Watanabe, Mio
Watson, Rachel E
Wei, Jierui
Weidner, Sarah
West, Patricia A.
Wiener, Matthew
Wilk, Julia M.
Williams, Sean L.
Winkel, Jane Hope
Wolford, Juliet Elizabeth
Wong, Elaine Wong
Wong, Lok Wai
Wu, You
Wu, Yuhan
Wu, Zhaojie
Xu, Jie
Xu, Siying
Yamada, Yoriyuki
Yan, Keyu
Yan, Shuo
Yang, Ran
Yang, Tianya
Yang, Wright
Yin, Mingyu
Yip, Melissa
Yoo, Seung Jong
Yoon, Hee-Yeun
You, Jayon
Yu, Helen
Yu, Jingran
Yu, Yin
Yuan, Ding
Yuan, Xiadong
Yuan, Xiaohuan
Zahn, Alexandra D.
Zellefrow, Donald A
Zeng, Chunlan
Zeng, Ying
Zhang, Liuyan
Zhang, Qing
Zhang, Wenmo
Zhang, Xiwei
Zhang, Yifang

Zhao, Yitian
Zheng, Huan
Zheng, Qinglan
Zheng, Xiao
Zhou, Jun
Zhu, Jianchun
Zhu, Yichen
Zhu, Yijia
Zolotorevskaya, Yelena

As we look to the future of the School and the discipline of landscape architecture, we asked alumni and faculty to reflect on their time at Penn, their work in design, their personal research, their teaching methodologies and their experiences as students, professors and practitioners. Their responses offer a diverse yet connected set of ideas about what Penn's legacy means and what is important for the future. Throughout these statements there is a sense that Penn, more than any other school, has been the incubator of landscape architecture's most important ideas and that this lays the groundwork for the 21st century as the profession of landscape architecture rises to its greatest challenges.

# FUTURE

## Tim Baird, M.L.A. '80

**What's your best memory of Penn and your manifesto now?**

I set out to accomplish two things in my professional career: to work with as many different designers as possible and to combine teaching with practice. I believe that the gulf that often separates the profession from the discipline can only be bridged by forging close relationships between the two. My contribution to this effort is to maintain a faculty position in the academy while simultaneously practicing. Teaching informs my practice and practice is integral to any success that I have in my teaching. Working closely with practitioners and understanding their needs is one way that the academy can remain relevant and the profession can evolve.

I have a slide of one of my favorite memories from my days at Penn but it has never been scanned and I have no idea where it resides today. For those too young to remember, a slide is an early form of image capture technology involving emulsion on a kind of plastic film with several tiny people inside black boxes that were called cameras but were nothing like what are referred to as cameras today. Toward the end of a party at Ian's farm after much food and drink, Laurie began to dance in the lawn with Victoria. Carol was in the house at the time so Ian, not to be outdone, grabbed the nearest small farm animal, a goat, held it to his chest, and danced away!

## Alan Berger, M.L.A. '90

**You are now leading your own research agenda at MIT. What do you owe to Penn in terms of your intellectual and creative development?**

Since the birth of environmentalism in the 1960s, Penn landscape architects and regional planners in search of ecological meaning for their work were taught to challenge market-driven economic paradigms of nature in lieu of a higher equilibrium for our built-natural environment. Think back to how Ian McHarg's science and research-based process for design sought to resist conventional economic thinking and unrelenting political pressures that threaten collective, long-term, incremental and sustainable planning. In order to do this, design and research were taught inseparably. It was thought that a common language and knowledge derived from understanding ecological processes, scientific principles, and regional systems percolated down through all types of practice and scales of thinking about landscape. McHarg's research reminds us that the greatest plans embody longevity and collective intelligence, which are defendable and resilient through turbulence.

But times change and so do professions. Over the past decade scientific research has all but vanished in landscape architecture. Landscape architecture faculties produce an embarrassingly low average of 0.34 scholarly publications annually per faculty member. There is relatively little or no externally funded research throughout the United States in some of the most acclaimed landscape architecture programs, including at Penn.

In a recent essay, ecologist David Orr explained the marginalization of McHargian research methods by attributing several reasons to why the culture of design and landscape architecture has abandoned scientific and rational research. This includes the hold of reductionism, the detriment of commodifying the natural world, and deeply misguided shortcomings of political process and decision-making that are largely guided by economics

and market forces. Ironically, these are all forces McHarg fought voraciously against!

The Department of Landscape Architecture and Regional Planning (as it was known in the 1990s when I was there) was still teaching students of landscape architecture to understand the environment holistically, to question conventional economic reality, but to also be critical always, of design culture itself in order to make it better. The rich diversity of faculty scientists, anthropologists, designers, and planners, working together to solve big scale problems fostered an intellectual environment that required competing perspectives to become inclusive and not sequestered into 'design' or 'research.' This, in essence, was how we were taught to conceive alternative worldviews, to understand how seeds of innovation are germinated, and to resist rote academic and professional protocols. This was the deep value of a Penn landscape architecture education that carried us over time through the daily grind and mundane aspects of practice.

Techniques of research in wide use throughout the physical design fields today were born at Penn during the 1970s, 1980s and 1990s, and included some of the first forms of mapping data and environmental phenomena, including the emergence of

geographic informational systems thinking. Through the use of mapping and other forms of measurement and visualization we discovered and revealed landscape capacities that others couldn't materialize with conventional tools or practice. Our own methods were inspired by looking outside of design toward fields of scientific inquiry for inspiration and rational methods for legitimacy, with additional fields for aesthetics and artistic ambitions. The school's great leaders crossed over the imaginary lines of landscape architecture, planning, science, anthropology, engineering, art, and ethics. McHarg, for example, cut through the skins separating the scientists and practitioners to argue for global acceptance of environmental suitability protocols. Anne Whiston Spirn laid the foundation for a renaissance of urban ecological principles in design teaching. James Corner and Anu Mathur gave a voice to inventive and imaginary phenomena and ecological process and entropy in design.

Penn's intellectual anchoring for the landscape architecture field relied on scientific thinking, which extensively echoed and honed the great cultural ambition of landscape as a 'public medium' over the 20th century. As a recent study of the field points out, the landscape profession was at its most influential when it was aligned with the influential environmental and social thinkers of its time, and it was most irrelevant when it was not.

Sadly, landscape architecture has drifted away from collaborative, well-funded, academic research towards practice-based education. The landscape 'academe' is drifting and anchorless, which is a cause for major concern. Landscape departments have handed over much of their teaching to practice-based education. Today it is common to find many schools with more than half of their faculty part-time practitioners, with little skill and capacity to conduct research, let alone scientifically qualified and peer-reviewed research. This problem viciously self perpetuates: as less research funding is attracted and awarded to landscape architectural educators, less funding is available to hire full-time faculty, so part-timers become permanent gap-fillers populating the system. Part-time faculty and practitioners are not invested in academic research, funded or otherwise, and they must work within their own constraints and billing regimes where little research can be accomplished in their project realizations. In the end, this scenario produces landscape architecture programs that either become quasi trade schools, training grounds for firms, or fold under economic pressure within the university system. Landscape architecture education is at an

important crossroad, if not crisis. The fragility of landscape's au currant thickens even further when one considers that past grand eras of designing with landscape as a 'public medium,' are now fiscally challenged by the age of austerity, economic efficiency, and shriveling public finances.

Landscape architecture could recognize this as a threat to its legacy and prepare itself for a major offensive surge of solid research to re-legitimize its cultural importance. Landscape architecture's future will only flourish if we can argue for it at the most basic levels of political and economic decision-making. Designers want to make things. This is our strength. We should strive to create a new type of design research whose goal is to create landscapes that emerge out of scientifically grounded principles and economic responsibility.

Sitting within the Graduate School of Fine Arts throughout most of the century, Penn's landscape architecture department had deep connections to the arts. It would be appropriate then to argue that Penn Design is the place for landscape architecture to form a renewed bridge, of the arts to the sciences. As the list below reveals, limiting landscape architecture to either visual arts or social sciences, or for design theory alone, will compete for the two smallest cuts of all research funding in universities.

This is a low ambition that nobody should endorse. The other alternative is collaborating with the sciences to obtain a larger part of the research pie. The latter requires a minimum level of research competence, which our schools neglect to teach and encourage.

Total funding at academic institutions for research in science/engineering:

$54.9 billion

Percentage breakdown:
life sciences-medical/bio/agriculture (60%)
engineering (15.7%)
physical (7.8%)
environmental science (5.4%)
social science (3.8%)

Total Funding for non-science/engineering:

$2.4 billion

Percentage breakdown:
education (38%)
journalism/law/social work (15%)
business (14%)
humanities (11%)
visual + performing arts (3%)

Penn's landscape architecture department could begin its second century with a revolutionary thrust into environmental work, informed by science, that drives new political change and entrenches landscape architecture back to its rightful place as a holistic, collectively responsible field aimed at improving the world's natural and built systems through intelligent and well-informed design. Penn's landscape research once expanded the profession's cultural influence, and it will again in its next century.

## Anita Berrizbeitia

**Could you comment on the qualities you experienced at Penn that are important to you?**

I arrived at Penn in the fall of 1998 and had the great honor of serving, for eleven years, in a department that was at the epicenter of a renaissance in landscape architecture. Innovation in the field had been a long-standing tradition at Penn, and in addition to McHarg, Spirn, Tomlin, and Olin, new paragons of the field were there: Hunt, Corner, and Mathur brought a wonderfully rich diversity of methods, visions, and concepts that took the ecological and design frameworks for which Penn was well known into new relevance. As a young faculty member, this was an extremely fertile ground in which to explore my own interests

in contemporary landscape architecture and urbanization in North and South America. Although there was a clear structure to the curriculum, there was also ample room to explore topics and sites well beyond the confines of the typical requirements of landscape architectural education in the US. I took advantage of this spirit of open inquiry and ventured into places that required the invention of new methods of design. The US-Mexico border, an ancient agricultural landscape in the Mediterranean, the reinterpretation of a paradigmatic modern public park in Caracas at a moment of significant political upheaval, are a few examples of the range of topics that were possible to explore at Penn. And what made this possible was in no small measure the continuous dialogue between the faculty, the commitment to engagement through teaching as an extension of research, and what seemed to be a never-ending level of energy everywhere. John, Laurie, Jim, Anu: I remain forever grateful.

It will indeed be a hard act to follow. Landscape architecture still enjoys significant cultural relevance. But the world continues to change at even greater speeds, and in ways we cannot predict. The challenge remains: to transform and advance the field at a pace that responds to the opportunities and the risks we, as a society, face. Unless we move from the generic to the specifically instrumental, and at the same time from the invisible to the experiential, landscape architecture will return once again to the realm of the merely mundane.

## Dilip da Cunha

**In partnership with Anu Mathur your research and practice resists the unreflexive use of convention to manufacture landscape architecture.**

**You also teach what I think could be described as landscape philosophy. Could you describe your current research and why you think it is important?**

Design to us is rooted in the possibility that people do not just see things differently but see different things. They constitute and visualize beyond the limits of language and beyond the disciplines that frame landscape design practice and discourse, particularly history and ecology. To some this act of constituting things is a metaphysical operation;

to us it is design imagination. It opens to question the 'things' that we take for granted, oftentimes as 'natural' entities. It also opens a more fundamental starting point for design particularly in places with a legacy of contention and imposition such as those in the wake of colonialism of one form or another.

We are currently working on the possibility that rivers in India, but elsewhere as well, exist by design. They are products of a particular articulation of the earth surface that presumes the separation of water from land and the confinement of this water within lines. Indeed, the idea that water flows from source or sources to sea is inseparable from the image of two lines or banks that begin in a point or points on high ground and run to the coast. Yet these lines cannot be taken for granted as universal. They are products of a cultivated sensibility, a particular literacy through which water is read, written and drawn on the earth surface, on paper, and in the imagination.

There is much to admire in these lines, especially in where, how and why they are drawn; but there is also the possibility that there are other ways to read, write, draw and imagine the earth surface, ways that may serve us better in a time when rivers are overdrawn, polluted, constrained, and, not least, the cause of increasing social and political conflict. In "The Invention of Rivers", the tentative title of an exhibition and book, we explore the art and craft of these lines, which from their humble foundations in the banks of rivers reach up to hold and support lofty ideas like city and civilization, but also earthy taken-for-granted realities such as valleys, floodplains, watersheds, dams and drains. Taking down this towering edifice exposes not just its foundation in the line of the river bank; it also reveals a terrain that can be engaged differently, such as through rain that is everywhere before it is 'water' somewhere.

On a more specific level we are pursuing the possibility that Ganga is a rain terrain, a world apart from the river Ganges, which is the confined linear geographic entity that underlies histories, ecologies and current planning and design agendas. Ganga, we suggest, is a complex temporal terrain, another ground upon which to anchor a new imagination and develop a vocabulary with which to articulate India's past, present, and future.

Our previous books and associated public exhibitions—"Mississippi Floods", "Deccan Traverses", and "Soak"—likewise seek to change the ground of design by including this ground in the act of design. These projects are part of what we do as designers; they are the activist side of our practice that seeks to expand design discourse not merely within the field of design but in

the public domain, for design we believe is not a privileged enterprise for the privileged but one that underlies everyday practices and conversations. Importantly, while our books and exhibitions work to change the public imagination and conversation they also create the opportunity to demonstrate through specific design interventions the efficacy of an alternative ground on which to situate the many intractable issues confronting societies today, including flood, sea-level rise, slums, and water scarcity.

The classes I teach, whether studios, lectures or seminars, open students to various ways by which we can question the vocabulary of design and the visualizing and representational regimes that have given us the 'things' that we take for granted, things ranging from river to region, plant to city, individual to nation. We look at various efforts through which these things have been systematized, programmed, argued, interrogated, and designed into the image and imagination; and we look for ways to cultivate a new imagination and open new possibilities for and though design projects.

Jill Desimini, M.L.A. & M.Arch. '05

**What values motivate you as a landscape architectural educator?**

I am committed to making great urban landscapes and teaching budding landscape architects to be responsible designers and stewards of the urban environment. I remember approaching then-chair James Corner as a 501 architecture student who just realized that landscape architecture was actually the career I was interested in as someone trying to find a way to design urban public space. He explained that architects may be actors but that landscape architects are more like directors, who guide processes to design and affect change. I was sold and have loved the discipline ever since.

I am trying to use design and ecology to help us reimagine cities with growing inventories of abandoned land, abandoned land that is home to increasingly rich and novel ecosystems. I am committed to exploring trans-disciplinary approaches to address a range of issues (including jobs, crime, storm water and pollution) through the manipulation and management of urban land. I am working toward design approaches that go beyond things like food production and park construction to address broader land uses. I am looking at how we perceive property and human occupation, and at how those perceptions affect our urban ecologies. How can we create value in abandoned urban spaces that are not perceived as valuable? How can we move beyond traditional market-driven value approaches?

The answers, for me, have to do with landscape innovation. We can't continue to define cities merely in terms of population loss. Landscape architecture has the potential to reverse this burden, and advocate for the value and opportunity that this land already offers, even if we don't measure that value, much less see it. Designers are positive thinkers with creative energies capable of imagining and articulating visionary futures. Designers can reframe our perceptions, they can project viable, environmentally and socially responsible alternatives. For me, design is not as much about fancy materials and expensive schemes as it is about being strategic, doing the most with the least number of moves. Landscape architecture can help us look at our older cities in a completely new way.

Raffaella Fabiani
Giannetto, M.L.A. '99

**Could you explain why it is so important that contemporary designers have a working knowledge of history?**

While it is true that much of the contemporary discourse and production of landscape architecture today lacks historical depth, some notable exceptions remind us why it is so important that contemporary designers have a working knowledge of history.

In his "Treatise on the Theory and Practice of Landscape Gardening Adapted to North America" (1844), Andrew Jackson Downing wrote that, "To attempt the smallest work in any art, without knowing either the capacities of that art, or the schools, or modes, by which it has previously been characterized, is but to be groping about in a dim twilight, without the power of knowing, even should we be successful in our efforts, the real excellence of our production; or of judging its merit, comparatively, as a work of taste and imagination." Downing's incisive remarks effectively summarize why historical knowledge is important for the practice and criticism of landscape architecture. His words were probably inspired by the fact that he was not only among the first professional landscape architects in America, but also that he happened to live and work in a country with a recently formed national identity which looked at the past of the Old World for clues about the best way to represent the American character and ideals. The history of garden making and landscape architecture continued to be valued until the dawn of Modernism, when the achievements of previous generations—described in purely stylistic terms, would be seen simply as a crippling form of nostalgia, hindering the progress of the discipline, and would be therefore dismissed. Garret Eckbo, for example, rejected the formal principles of the past, above all the axis, which, he claimed had 'ran out of gas in the 17th century.' The importance of history resurfaced at the close of the twentieth century not only because designers felt disenchanted with the unfulfilled promises of Modernism and the

limits of the eco-fundamentalism that followed, but also because history has come to be understood as encompassing more than a simple account of historical styles, and gardens and designed landscapes of the past have been discussed in the context of material culture, social studies, gender and reception histories. It is surprising, however, that a few contemporary landscape architects wonder about the usefulness of a sound historical knowledge of their own discipline, still clinging, anachronistically, to Modernist arguments.

"It is both astonishing and even amusing"—says John Dixon Hunt in his most recent book—"to see some modern landscape architects seemingly or deliberately forget past endeavors in their wish to push the envelope of their profession . . . Turning a blind eye to earlier work can give any architect the advantage of fresh creativity." But if, as Hunt maintains, "historians may," "with hindsight, trace the latent antecedents of current work," then, I wonder, what is the meaning of that supposedly advantageous, but amnesic point of departure and how seriously are we going to assess its final product?

Design is a creative process—it has to do with invention, meaning the creation of something new or at least different from what already exists. We praise designers whose marks of distinction are their

own inventive minds, but does that mean that they invent out of nothing? Of course not. Invention is one of two words that translate into English the Latin term inventio. The other word for inventio is inventory. This modern English term points to the gathering and ordering of numerous and varied materials, which, in our discipline, are made up of precedents, together with the ideas that have inspired them and the discourses that have emerged from them. And this inventory may come handy whether we are dealing with an intimidating blank slate or an overwhelmingly rich historic site. Calling attention to the roots of invention reminds us of a fundamental truth about the nature of creativity, that is that having an 'inventory' is, in fact, a fundamental requisite for 'invention'.

One may argue that a working knowledge of landscape architectural history is useful to the extent in which a designer is asked to work on historic sites, where he/she is forced to dialogue with earlier cultural traces. But this is not the case. As a young landscape architecture student at Penn reminds us, "An understanding of techniques and tendencies, both recent and more dated, can aid the modern designer in clarifying his or her own intentions, organizations, and strategies." On this subject, Laurie Olin in reference to his firm's design for Wagner Park [criticizing an earlier proposal to adopt a neoclassical plan] writes, "Since it was no longer the sixteenth century, I saw no reason to create a sixteenth-century layout . . . The world was different now from that of the seventeenth- and nineteenth-century gardens; it was New York at the end of the twentieth century, and a lot had changed. In a search for ways to break up the static classical forms and in response to the need of unifying the elements of the plan I seized on the Renaissance Revival plan of the Conservatory garden from the 1930s and set to work transforming it and pulling it apart, rearranging the pieces . . ." Olin's use of historical precedent, in this case an early botanic garden, as both point of departure and form of contrast, and his understanding of its inappropriate application on a highly urbanized and exposed landfill along the Hudson River, allowed him to further clarify his intention and the role of a new public landscape in a specific and twentieth-century context. As Olin's insight indicates, history, by allowing us to understand what we aren't, may allow us to further clarify what we are.

The value of historical research for the landscape architecture profession can hardly be overemphasized. Understanding how garden and landscape history has been written and received, how it has been appropriated, or simply acknowledged and rewritten through design allows us

to understand ourselves and our place in the world and without this capacity, as A. J. Downing once noted, we would be groping about in a dim twilight.

## Lindsey Falck

**Could you reflect on why you think our appreciation of materiality of landscape is so important for designers?**

When one leaves the heat, noise and car-fumes of the city streets and enters the courtyard of Seville Cathedral there is an immediate sense of relief, followed by more slowly absorbed additional sensory rewards of the place.

One's eyes are focused on the overall beauty of the place, the shaded courtyard of low-pruned orange trees, the fountain spilling water over the lip of its bowl into the under-foot water channels, the meticulously laid cobble stones of the paving, and, of course, the quiet dignity of the enclosing buildings on the perimeter of the courtyard.

One's ears pick up the sounds of the moving water. One's nose picks up the subtle scent of the orange blossom of the trees. One's feet feel the texture of the rough-tooled faces of the granite cobble stones.

All the senses are affected by the detail design of the "hard" and "softer" elements of the design, within the overall concepts that generated the space some hundreds of years ago.

To create spaces like this courtyard one has to have a working knowledge of the characteristics of the materials to be used, how they will look, feel, sound, smell when installed, and how they will mature with response to weather and use over time.

One also has to know how and where the materials and plants will be acquired, processed, and installed with the tools and skills of the masons, carpenters, landscape workers, and others who leave their marks on the design elements.

The more close-up and hands-on of the experience of the designers, the more likely they are to provide rewarding places for human use and occupation.

## David Gouverneur

**You have a background in architecture and urban design and your research focuses on informal settlements. How has your time at Penn influenced your approach to contemporary urbanism?**

Through my time at Penn and based on my experience with cities in the global south I have become increasingly interested in what I refer to as 'informal armatures'.

What this means is that the designer attends to the provision of infrastructure (both hard and soft) as the catalyst for growth but the designer does not expect, or attempt to control the actual growth. This is a method I have been testing in my design studios and it is one I believe well suited to informal settlements—places

we used to call slums, places where over 2 billion of the world's population now live.

Some aspects of my approach are embedded in the orthodox field of urban design but I have found that a landscape architectural approach brings significant differences to urban design. Firstly, there is a better understanding of the natural-territorial substrate that defines the location, performance, and general morphology of cities and districts. Secondly, landscape architects focus on the performative, qualitative and aesthetic qualities of open space as the organizer of urban form, which has the ability to manage, in a holistic manner, the relations between infrastructure, mobility and water management, etc. Landscape architects are also good as shifting scale and linking from the regional to the site specific scale and are open to designing places which are intentionally left somewhat open ended so they can adapt to change. I find that a landscape architectural approach to urbanism is also more inclusive of both cultural and ecological differences and allows me to think in a holistic but at the same time focused manner.

However, in what has emerged as landscape urbanism or ecological urbanism there is also a tendency to minimize the importance of strategic planning, the participation of urban actors, and ignore the regulatory aspects of urban infill affecting building and block typologies, and so on. Landscape urbanism overlooks these real conditions as overly prescriptive, rigid, non-process oriented and lacking morphological and aesthetic value. In my work I am trying to find a balance between the open-ended catalytic approach and the overly prescriptive. I would also like to voice my strong belief in cross-disciplinary work, something which I have carried out during my career and which I have been able to set forward at PennDesign through studio work and elective courses. Landscape architecture's capacity for interdsciplinarity and its systematic and holistic approach to urbanism are why it is so well placed to play a major role in the formulation of cities this century.

Andrea Hansen, M.L.A., M.Arch. '10

**As an emerging academic, how do you see the future of landscape architectural education?**

My path to academia was strongly influenced by the Penn landscape program's commitment to independent thinking and research. The studios I took, whether at the 500-level or the 700-level, struck just the right balance between didactic and open: being informed but not restricted by the pedagogies of critics as diverse as Anuradha Mathur and Nanako Umemoto. This balance made independent inquiry on the part of the student seem valued, and I relished the opportunity to propose ideas of my own, which I admit often strayed from the syllabus. Nevertheless, my critics treated these sometimes-divergent ideas with thoughtful criticism. Though I was not fully aware of it until post-graduation ('hindsight is 20/20' is never more true than in the case of the overworked design student), the criticism I received in studios helped inform a coherent design and research trajectory that culminated in a thesis. In fact, my thesis was developed specifically to revisit many of the sites and themes of my previous landscape and architecture studios.

The thesis, entitled "Fluxscape: Remapping Philadelphia's Post-Industrial Terrain", benefited from an interdisciplinary perspective I attribute to Penn's seamlessly-integrated dual-degree program — I studied landscape architecture and architecture concurrently, though having begun my graduate education in the landscape program, my architectural projects were always strongly influenced by site context, ecology, and shifting topologies. I was able to draw from these interests and received valuable feedback from advisors in both programs, and the thesis ended up taking on a hybrid, infrastructural character that operated at the urban and regional scale. In fact, the thesis themes of relational mapping and infrastructural interventions for vacant land in post-industrial cities continue to form the backbone of my research today.

I find independent research opportunities such as independent study, seminars, and thesis to be critical components of landscape architecture education today.

This is particularly true as landscape architecture as a discipline seeks to broaden its scope from a practice-driven field with roots in aristocratic garden design to a research-driven field capable of tackling complex infrastructural and remediation projects and being important voices in municipal, national, and global policy. To ensure that students are able to add to this discourse, I believe it is crucial for them to begin to form an individual agenda from day one of their education. Whether students end up in practice or academia, engaged at the micro or macro scale, or focused on formal, ecological, or urban issues (or a combination of the three as is most often the case), their education necessarily must concern itself not only with exposing students to the range of issues and scales that face landscape architects, but also with stepping back so that students can have the freedom to form their own opinions. This was certainly the case for me at PennDesign.

Ron Henderson, M.L.A. '95

**What was it that attracted you to Penn?**

In 1991, I attended an open house for prospective students—at Harvard. I had been accepted into the landscape architecture program there and went to hear the speaker that evening, Glenn Murcutt, whose inspiring discourse on "the -ings of things" gave a powerful voice to working, talking, eating—to living—with each other and to listening, seeing, touching—again, to living—with the non-human world. Thanks to Harvard's invitation to Glenn at that open house, I decided that I would attend Penn, where Glenn was teaching.

Anne Spirn was chair and she had invited Glenn to teach in the landscape architecture department.

With Anne Spirn and David Leatherbarrow, then chair of the architecture department, there was an environment of mutual respect and shared theory between the two departments at Penn that was uncommon then—and remains rare in design schools today.

## Alison Hirsch, P.h.D., MS, M.L.A. '11

**You seem to have a great love for what you do. What motivates you as a practitioner and a teacher?**

I had the privilege of an extended academic training at Penn while pursuing my PhD under the advisement of John Dixon Hunt and my MLA under the leadership of James Corner and Anu Mathur. This combination of mentors provided not just the tools and techniques to be a capable scholar and designer, but placed invaluable emphasis on methods of working and creative thinking, which are fundamental to intellectual inquiry and pursuit.

With John, I discovered history—not as a sealed record of the past—but, like landscape, something alive and constantly renegotiated through new interpretation and frames of reference. This is not only integral to the practice of writing, an essential component of landscape architecture, but to the act of shaping places which are inevitably latent with memories, histories and physical traces of time.

An understanding of history as creative process and interpretive inquiry was enriched by the rigors of studio curriculum, which emphasized drawing (modeling, etc)—not merely as a vehicle of communication or demonstration— but as a critical and generative act that unleashes new questions and provokes new readings of sites as they are shaped. Like history, the practice of designing landscapes is not about reaching final design synthesis, but is an open and transformative process that prompts new understandings and ideas of what it means to dwell in the world.

As new faculty in a younger landscape architecture department, my experience at Penn shapes how I conduct courses, structure curriculum and challenge my students to revel in the process and act of creative inquiry and exploration. As co-founder of a fledgling practice with my partner, who I met undergoing the same rigors of Penn Design training, we are constantly building on the tremendous footing Penn provided and engaging in conversations stimulated by this dynamic base.

## Keith Kaseman

**Your studios take risks with method and encourage formal experimentation in gnarly sites— what are you chasing with these studios and how does it relate to your practice?**

Specifically configured to employ high levels of design experimentation as the primary fuel for new modes of creative exchange in relation to future space in the city, the consistent pursuit within my LARP studios has been to project questions and ambitions into spatial potentials yet to be imagined. In this light, design agility is framed as a prime urban reconnaissance tool with which we may construct new configurations to think through, intended to help us leap beyond the imminent mediocrity typically embedded within most municipal strategies shaping up on the horizon. As such, these are not research studios in the traditional sense, but rather operate as semi-systematic spatial think-tanks wholeheartedly concerned with design as a proactive urban tactic, and high fidelity as the means through which spatial action and demonstration may spark new forms of exchange. In other words, the ambition is always to play through a multitude of questions, ideas, strategies and potential configurations in order to imagine alternate courses for the city's future through refined spatial engagement. One way to supercharge the chase is to focus on and operate through 'gnarly sites', extracting and constructing their latent capacity to spark and propagate an exploratory mindset that at least leans towards radical from the outset. While many factors interweave in order for a 'site' to qualify as gnarly, the minimum criterion couples improbability with urgency. Gnarly sites help us confidently claim that if we don't rigorously pursue this completely overlooked potential as a source for deep and impactful transformations of the city, nobody will.

By orchestrating dynamic internal exchanges within the studio and engaging an extremely wide array of people outside of the studio and from a broad spectrum of creative, civic and professional realms through key mixer-sessions, we can guarantee that a wide array of questions will amplify the diversity of spatial pursuits. Working through physical, digital and strategic space more or less simultaneously along the way, the fundamental goal of this studio experimentation is to play through space and demonstrate high-fidelity urban imaginaries. This is exactly how we frame the operational standards of our professional experimental design practice as well, which has excitingly evolved in parallel with my studio participation at Penn.

Niall Kirkwood, M.L.A. '85

**How has your design philosophy been shaped by your education at Penn?**

I had the good fortune to grow up in the cultural environment of Scotland where I found quite simply—the power of geology and engineering in the landscape. If there is one place, one country in the world in which to understand the processes and identity of human place, design and landscape in creation and construction, that secret unity of the artificial and the natural, landscape and architecture then surely it must be here. It is a hard and practical country— and that is the fault of both its latitude and geography. It was this background that Ian McHarg brought to the Department of Landscape Architecture and infused us all with his deep attachment to education in the general sense and in particular, to our understanding of the natural world, as well as improvement to the environments in which people lived and worked, and of the processes by which people produced what they need. The concept of improvement meant an interest in history and change, but also to the physical world itself where change was involved at every stage, whether in an understanding of physics and chemistry or the much slower processes discovered in geology. I emerged from Philadelphia concerned with the mastery and mystery of landscape craft and art, the beauty and elegance of formal structure, and a search for the authentic in the built landscape. The basis of my approach to design is philosophical reflection on the nature of landscape, place and people then action, the humanistic idea of an all-inclusive re-construction of the world through an engagement with the ordinary physical environment appropriate to the scale of endeavor and using the physical and economic means at our disposal. It is still as valid today as it was then.

## Chris Marcinkowski

**Can you describe your current research and how this relates to the phenomenon of rapid global urbanization?**

The last 15 years have seen a rapid proliferation globally of speculative urbanization (housing, infrastructure, cultural amenities, etc.) in a range of political, economic and geographic contexts. Countries as diverse as the United States, Ireland, Iceland, Panama, Angola, Turkey, Algeria and the United Arab Emirates have all experienced (or are currently experiencing) rapid expansions of their urbanized territories predicated on presumptions of continuous economic expansion and population growth. China in particular has been under increased scrutiny of late as a

growing number of media reports and images emerge of massive, unoccupied new settlement being built in the country's interior western and southern provinces. However, perhaps the most dramatic example of the potential consequences of the speculative tendencies of contemporary urbanization, both in terms of its scale and the repercussions of its failure, can be found in Spain.

From 1998-2008, Spain experienced an unprecedented expansion of its urbanized territory. Madrid, for example, nearly doubled its total urbanized footprint during this period. Much of this investment in development can be traced back to three political events, including the Land Law of 1998; the introduction of the euro in 2002 (with its corresponding reduction in interest rates); and the liberalization of labor constraints that same year. These policy decisions, in companion with the perceived successes of the 1992 Barcelona Olympics and Seville Expo as reproducible urban regeneration strategies, led to a radical over-privileging of urbanization within the Spanish economy. The result was nearly 20 percent of Spain's GDP being devoted to construction-related industries at the peak of this period—nearly four times the proportion seen in the U.S. and the U.K., whose economies both saw contemporaneous development bubbles—and a rate just below the 30 percent of GDP currently conservatively estimated for China. Although held up in the first decade of the 21st century as a global exemplar of both economic policy and design innovation, Spain's urban growth agenda over this period led directly to the precipitous state of the country's current economy.

There is a clear body of evidence of design's complicity—whether intentional or not—in the production of this particular moment in history. In fact, I would argue that the recent proliferation globally of incomplete, and abandoned urban settlement can be traced to a widespread disciplinary reliance on the inflexible, singular formats of settlement and easily replicable urban spatial products that characterize current urbanization.

Given the increasing reliance on urbanization as a primary instrument of economic production in both emerging and established economies, there is a clear need for the urban design disciplines engaged in this work to reconsider their particular modes of operation; the tools upon which they rely; and the metrics by which the success of these projects are evaluated, in order to begin anticipating and negotiating the inevitable instability that stems from contemporary urbanization.

In this context, no primary urban design discipline is more readily prepared to negotiate this uncertain urban future than landscape architecture. As the only discipline that fundamentally embraces contingency as a core capacity, landscape architecture has a unique facility to navigate the demands of an urban future characterized by constantly evolving pressures of the near, interim and long-term. Yet despite this capacity, the disciplinary opportunity implied by the phenomenon described above has yet to be fully embraced. As such, there remains a unique occasion to expand landscape architecture's agency by actively reclaiming territory and scope related to this work from other allied disciplines that currently find themselves in various states of intellectual crisis.

In particular, I would advocate that landscape architecture think bigger as a discipline—literally—and endeavor to recapture its physical and regional planning progeny lost over the last 60 years in order to expand landscape architecture's role in shaping the urban future. This is by no means a suggestion to abandon physical, material and experiential design; rather, it is a call to develop new landscape forms and strategies that are more fully hybridized with the varying physical and systemic demands of current urbanization.

At the same time, landscape architecture should endeavor to become more nimble, looking to develop innovative tactics related to discrete interventions that have the capacity to catalyze larger systemic transformations. In this way, the work of the discipline operates simultaneously at the macro-scale of the big vision or strategy, as well as at the local scale of engagement. Such an approach invites interpolation between the two scales of work that can more readily negotiate the volatility of contemporary urbanization.

In order to begin operating in this way, landscape architecture must actively embrace systems of politics and economics as they relate to urbanization as enthusiastically as the more familiar ecological and environmental concerns. In this vein, the true potential of the discipline lies in engaging bigger, more complex, more consequential urban topics from both the macro-strategic scale, concurrent with the more nimble local scale. Global agriculture; the management of water rights; planning and design of new settlement; desertification and corollary regimes of reforestation; alternative energy production; natural resource extraction; sea-level rise; or the accommodation of displaced or refugee populations all represent fertile areas of prospective operation for this kind of work.

At this particular moment in time, landscape architecture remains ascendant primarily because today's dominant cultural interests so nicely intersect with the discipline's established interests. Yet, to maintain such a trajectory beyond the present and to avoid the risk of becoming a discipline engaged only with first-world amenity-driven urban projects, landscape architecture must move beyond defining itself based on typologies of the past, and look to reorient its concerns toward actively shaping the global urban future.

## Anurandha Mathur, M.L.A. '91

**You have seen a lot of change at Penn. What do you think is of real importance for its future as a great program?**

When I came to Penn, first as a student and then faculty, the field was still polarized between ecology and art. This was the status quo— the way practices and schools were differentiated. I was hired at Penn as someone who could bridge this divide. In many ways I did not accept this separation. Designers and critics were already looking to use ecology artfully in design and to bring design into ecological planning. As an architect from India, having studied under teachers like B. V. Doshi and having worked with Minnette De Silva in Sri Lanka— ecology and art to me were not separable to begin with.

I believe Anne Spirn intuitively understood this and put her faith in a new generation of designers who had studied at Penn when she hired Jim and then me on the faculty. What was significant about the new curriculum that was initiated soon after under John Dixon Hunt's tenure as chair, was that we decided to change the subject. We moved away from a moralistic and positivist posture to an idea of design accommodating a critical reading of nature, culture, and history. John positioned the idea of the picturesque not as an application but a critical movement against a status quo while Jim challenged the taken for granted European precedents in landscape and brought an appreciation of the measures of the ordinary American landscape with a fresh visual palette. It was an exciting time of experimentation and ferment. Looking back at the brochure I designed to announce the new curriculum the phrase 'Inquiries in Process' that we collectively coined still captures for me our aspiration for the field. We said at the time that "landscape architecture at Penn is then doubly about process—the complex and dynamic processes by which sites from gardens to regions are formed; and the process whereby a student learns a discipline – through visual acuity, drawing, history and theory." I still hold this to be true.

I believe that the greatest achievement of the program was not in any concrete position, method, or formulation, but a belief in landscape architecture as an open and dynamic inquiry even if it meant the demise of the profession as we know it. In order to instrumentalize this aspiration we were motivated to sustain an emphasis and conversation on ideas and technique, on situation and invention, on the agency of drawing and visualization as a means to open the imagination, as well as a critique and awareness of the power of representation and history especially in a post-colonial milieu. The latter reading of landscape in particular is an emphasis that Dilip and I brought to the program.

In the past few years I have seen a return at Penn to an uncritical acceptance of the language of ecology, planning and spectacle that pervades the profession. The projective, generative, and speculative acts of drawing and making are too easily taken over by image-making that positions itself as being more real, more objective, and more immediate. I can see this being a response to, on the one hand, the developer's 'investment' agenda that has consumed a large part of the profession and, on the other hand, problems that present opportunities and give satisfaction that only problem-solving can; or perhaps it is a consequence of the tools we use (mouse vs pencil; program vs labor). More importantly there is an erosion of vigilance and dialogue on what constitutes generative work, creativity, and inquiry. Today, this is more crucial than ever before, particularly given that we operate on a global stage. As a University we should not be in the business of transferring 'best practices' to all places on earth without the tools, techniques, and most importantly, milieu to question our most fundamental assumptions.

**The 501 studio you and Dilip da Cunha teach is well known for its emphasis on situated representation. What have you been trying to achieve with this studio?**

In our teaching of 501 over the last decade Dilip and I have engaged some enigmatic and marginal landscapes in the vicinity of Philadelphia as open terrains (rather than bounded sites) to introduce incoming students to design. Traversing these places— that have ranged from forests, bogs, urban creeks, successional infrastructural landscapes, and even historic garden's like Bartram's— has challenged us to extend taken for granted notions of space, time, history, and ecology.

We encourage our students to think of themselves as pioneers— the first on the scene—as they make their way and accumulate each week a sense of territory through measuring and other modes of drawing, photographing and investigating conditions and ideas that extend what is visible. These engagements, which we call 'traverses', introduce students to the conventions in drawing, modeling, photographing, and other ways of imaging and knowledge construction. They also open them to ways of pushing these conventions in order to capture much more than space, in particular, time, materiality, and movement. We realize, as they do, that places cannot be exhausted in their readings and can be walked differently each time. In that sense traversing in the field and in the studio is an act of both transgression and invention that demands choices to be made and selected conditions be drawn out. It provides them with a vocabulary of place, a vocabulary by which a terrain is measured, its story told, and its condition transformed.

Students figure out through their physical engagement in the field and in studio that the act of seeing, measuring and other ways of engaging place is already an act of design, or that design begins with how we stride, how we see, how we draw out a place. We inherited this studio as the 'path' project and in the spirit of Henry David Thoreau do not see 'path' as a line in a landscape or a means to get from here to there—

but as a process of engaging and constructing landscape. What set the landscape program at Penn apart from other design schools in the past and can today—is a sense of experimentation and invention in design practices and in situating design in the world.

Carol McHarg, M.L.A. '77

**What was it like being a student at Penn in the mid '70's?**

The Department of Landscape Architecture and Regional Planning in the mid-70s was an exciting place. Faculty and students were comrades engaged in implementing and fine-tuning a cutting edge approach to environmental salvation. Ian was our leader, our guru, and our messiah. He travelled the world, spreading the dogma of this new religion of ecological design and planning and the world was beginning to pay attention.

In Meyerson Hall faculty and students worked at a feverish pace developing new theories, new connections (personal and academic) and new attitudes to design and planning. We knew we

were at the right place at the right time and were happily devoted to learning how to save the world.

Even those of us who came from liberal arts backgrounds knew we were engaged in something groundbreaking and were willing to suffer for this privilege. 20 hours a day in the studio—no problem. In fact, a breeze compared to the frequent and highly charged charrettes that demanded 30 hours a day.

I'll never forget our first presentation of 501. Most people worked in teams, but I had foolishly struck out on my own and was exceptionally nervous about explaining the geology of my site— shale hills and limestone valleys— to all those who probably knew a whole lot more then me. As it turned out, what I had to say didn't much matter because the faculty engaged in a ferocious war that consumed the entire day. I can't remember the subject, the sides or the outcome, but I do remember several students talked about transferring.

After all this work and all this tension, Fridays at five we all let loose. Happy hours were well known, well attended and highly regarded. It was here that many new connections were made and several led to permanent alliances including Ian and me, Vicky Steiger and Laurie Olin, Bob Hanna and

Beverly Briggs, and John Berger and Kit Wallace. This kind of 'faculty to student connecting' has since been outlawed, but it was de rigueur back then and when I graduated in 1977, I was not the only one who received a spouse along with a degree.

Karen M'Closkey and Keith VanDerSys

**Your studios and your practice are testing the potential of contemporary geometry made possible through computation to** generate new landscapes. Can you discuss how it functions as a generative tool which can achieve both surficial and structural change.

Recent digital media provide new ways to engage the temporal and relational qualities inherent to the dynamic medium of landscape by enabling us to explore what is intrinsic to all modes of visualization—the relationship between technique and ideation. For example, there are many models of change and process within landscape architecture, both in terms of how change is incorporated into design methods and how each mode of visualization supports an idea about how change is presumed to occur materially in the landscape itself. These include simultaneity (the superimposition of multiple images that convey a shifting landscape over time, as seen in the work of Mathur, Da Cunha); successional (sequential drawings to illustrate changes in landscape composition over time, as seen in the work of James Corner Field Operations); or episodic (notational drawings, such as Lawrence Halprin's eco-scores). In our work, we are interested in recursion as a model of change. This notion pertains to both the techniques enabled by computation (where sequences of operations are used to relate process and form through feedback) as well as to the resultant forms (i.e.: patterns).

We are interested in digital media for their role in the formation of landscapes rather than simply in the depiction of landscapes, which has been the dominant trend. The use of digital media in landscape architecture has remained largely within the realm of two-dimensional explorations that simply replicate manual drawing techniques, such maps, montages, or diagrams. Though all design is iterative (e.g.: manual drawing /modeling, then assessing, then altering, then reassessing, etc.), digital modeling expands the ability to relate quantitative and qualitative information. For instance, parametric software enables the modeling of numerical information in terms of force, quantity, and direction (such as in water or wind flow) in order to generate surfaces that are intrinsically relational; that is, entities are defined by virtue of their association or proximity to other elements. Consequently, the affiliation between form and process is inherent to the model; changes made to one entity have a reciprocal effect on neighboring entities. Flow, direction and quantity are linked to profile: if you change the flow, it alters the profile (i.e.: topography) and if you change the profile, it alters the flow. As a generative design tool, this type of modeling fosters the formation of new grounds, challenging how functions are 'assigned' to landscapes, in order to create new assemblages or new 'natures.'

Valerio Morabito

**You have great faith in drawing the landscape. Why is that? What are you trying to find when you draw?**

I believe that my drawing is a memory of the future. I have never drawn in front of a real landscape: urban, natural or industrial. I always draw it later, without having it in front of me. After some lines the drawings, which represents a landscape through memory, becomes a non precise visual perception you have to deal with. A different reality.

In my opinion this process of re-presentation is related with how a site could be different, how it could change. The site is alive in the sketch drawings and, processing the memory into its future, it avoids the present. The idea of the present

simply doesn't exist anymore, it disappears into the memory and its future.

In this way each sketch drawing analyzes reality and produces its design: in my mind the memory is made by spots, it is fragmented. For this reason my memory produces extensive blank spaces to be filled, voids in which the future stretches out inside them and fills them like water. My drawings do not have a predetermined technique but they choose one in relationship of the different sites they pretend to represent and then, after deciding the technique, they build precise rules by themselves: analog or digital the sketch drawings would like to compete with the speed of digital camera, controlling its photos to use them to create new relationships. When I change the site the technique changes and develops its rules. My drawing tries to avoid repetition and accepts mistakes: the best possible precision.

Afterwards a few sketches become paintings, although not in the common sense of the term, they become more like big sketches made on canvas - with oil, acrylic or ink colors - which seem like paintings; they are expressions of the contrast between the different scales of the technique, in terms of materials and shapes. Many times these drawings are not related to the design approach in my landscape projects, but they are exercises, short stories only written because I want to train my skills to write stories. This is a kind of poetic methodology of work. With this process the sketches wait to be used in a new space as projects, they are the Genius Loci, the second Genius Loci opposed to the Genius Loci of the site, able to deal with it in terms of morphology and poetry, geometry and illusion.

Ellen Neises, M.L.A. '02

**You are teaching studios that place an emphasis on large-scale systems and you teach a theory unit titled "Designed Ecologies". Can you explain what you are trying to achieve in your teaching and how you think it relates to the advance of the discipline and new forms of practice?**

One thing that has defined Penn and its diverse faculty is belief in the vitality and immensity of the landscape architectural project. In this school, designed landscapes have been understood as the means and grounds where, across cultures and time, humans have struggled with the art of settlement, with existential questions, with the nature of their own embodiment. Our medium is nature and, as McHarg wrote, "Nature contains the history of the evolution of matter, life, and man. It is the arena of past, present, and future. It exhibits the laws that obtain. It contains every quest that man can pursue. It tells every important story that man would know."

My studios and seminars explore ways to fulfill this outsized ambition and make the charisma of our medium more visible in the range of landscape architectural work being made today. In defining studio problems the last two years, I have been looking for openings for substantial change in longstanding arrangements of capital, policy, belief, material and experience— moments of instability or tipping points.

Through reading, conversation and design, we search for means to exploit the openings, staking out compelling problems that can be recast or resolved by design. We think across scales and concerns to enrich the content and nuance of projects.

They are strategic but also something more. The focus on non-equilibrium moments in complex, large-scale systems forces us to think about what landscape in particular can do, and expands the array of landscape design actions that may have agency. Our work is injected into the problem milieu with the aim of helping the players conceive alternative futures, increasing their appetite for quality and tolerance for risk.  I refer to this as 'imaginative ecology'—an exploration of the conceptual, artistic and scientific dimensions of the natural world as stimuli to design invention. It is a means of giving qualitative depth to strategic work and surpassing technocratic attention to landscape services.

My subject, "Designed Ecologies" looks at topics like change in population composition, devolution, punctuated equilibrium, and system adaptation from vantage points in biology, ecology, economics, social science, art and thermodynamics, and considers applications in design. When these sorts of sensibilities are brought to pressing problems of cities or regions, rigorously investigated, we can imagine potential for tremendous diversification of landscape architectural output. Potent examples of landscape-powered transformation will advance our own sense of possibility as well as perception of landscape architecture's capacity.

This is important to advance the field because, despite heightened awareness of ecological imperatives and opportunities, we have not yet claimed a place at the head of many tables. Architects and engineers are often seen by public clients as the people who bring high art and performance to 'green' pursuits. Planners, urban designers, environmentalists and sustainability experts are thought to be good at setting the rules of the game and 'getting to scale.' Policy people gauge what the political environment will endorse and wield the non-physical inputs. Ecologists, engineers, and real estate consultants define what works. Community engagement professionals establish dialog with residents of places that have become 'sites' to scope what should be designed. Artists examine nature through the lens of culture to produce interesting hybrids. Media designers convert change directions into zeitgeist.

Landscape architecture's strength as integrator of all of these domains, and as a key creator in most, must be more widely felt.

Cora Olgyay, M.L.A. '85

**You obviously enjoy teaching and yet your subject area is not easy to convey. How do you do it?**

When I was a student, the applicability of grading and site engineering to design was a mystery to me and to most my classmates.  I didn't understand the relevance until I took studios with the legendary Ed Bye. Ed approached design in an elegant and intuitive way. In his studios, sculpting the land was integral to the concept and development of the site design. I can still hear his soft, slow voice as his hands would gesticulate, describing and giving shape to a landform. I was smitten with the beauty and power of grading.

Grading is often considered a 'technical' subject: a series of calculations adjunct to the study of design practice and theory. I disagree completely. The calculations required to grade are incredibly basic; the real challenge is in how to use and apply the calculations to sculpt the land. The challenge is grading design, not grading calculations.

My goal in teaching is to make grading and site engineering immediately assessable as a design tool. We cover key topics with brief lectures and examples, followed by a series of in-class exercises to ensure that the material is understood and mastered. Our students work in groups, help each other, and ask questions. This is a great way to encourage exploration and collaboration, and to ensure competence. We further explore the design potential of the grading concepts with field trips, modeling assignments, and incorporating grading into the students individual studio projects.

Ours is a very interactive class. With a little push and encouragement, our students go from fearful to fearsome. They understand the importance of grading in their landscape projects, that landform is a way of developing and test their ideas and ensuring the viability of their concepts. A few years ago, after a particularly challenging session with a student working

to resolve their studio grading design, the student said "Oh, I get it: grading is just like design". I responded that grading is design.

Context and applicability are important in keeping grading relevant and central in our students' hectic lives. In teaching some of the more technical calculations, such as the Rational Formula and Mannings Equation, we pull the equations apart to see how we can use the variables in our designs. In this way, we can use the Roughness Coefficient, slope, soils and overland flow time to reduce the volume and rate of overland flow, not just to size stormwater systems. The 'wetted perimeter' variable in Mannings Equation is a great tool for slowing down water before it ever gets to a pipe.

I am a practicing landscape architect who is still fascinated by the transformation of ideas and drawings into built work. Grading design is a cornerstone in this process. Addressing issues of weather, water management, soils, erosion, circulation and access are core to the practice of landscape architecture, and our students should be beyond proficient. They should be poets.

## Laurie Olin

**You have intentionally kept one foot in the academy and one in practice without letting either compromise the quality of the other. How does this work for you?**

Soon after graduating from architecture school I entered practice in the firm conviction that it was a remarkable endeavor, the purpose of which was to improve the lot of society through the making of beautiful, functional and well built places, mostly buildings as I'd been trained. Later as demonstrated by my turning to landscape planning and design I shifted my interests, both broadening and deepening their subject and ambition, a lessening of involvement with objects and things and an increasing awareness of the relationships and arrangements of them, of settlement and community, of cities, the public realm and their relationship to ecology and the natural world which I had known when young.

It was during this period of mental, emotional, and artistic growth that I was first asked to teach by Richard Haag, one of my own teachers. Rich was a remarkable teacher who had opened a practice in Seattle while beginning his teaching career at the University of Washington. He engaged a number of his students to help in the fledgling office. It was stimulating and rewarding. We studied at school, and worked on real projects. We sat around, drank a bit of beer together and talked about all the things that seemed important in life and design. It was serious. It was fun. We were making gardens, parks, campuses, memorials, urban districts, while debating the ills of society and speculating about what we were reading and wished to turn our efforts toward.

Since that period with the exception of several breaks, each for a few years at a time (all before I was in my mid-thirties when I retreated to read, write, draw, paint, and sort myself out) I have been in practice, working full time on projects, many of which have been built in part if not completely. Also throughout this time I have taught at one university or another for a significant portion of the year.

It seems perfectly natural and somewhat necessary to me.

Why or how does this work? The purpose of professional schools is to educate and train individuals to become responsible professional practitioners or teachers of practitioners of some activity of importance and needed by society– whether it is medicine, law, architecture, landscape architecture, engineering, or some other discipline of difficulty and legal obligation in society. The point of it all concerns that which we can do for society, for others as well as ourselves. We are agents of change. We are builders. We are also dreamers. Dreamers of new methods and better designs, of a world improved somehow through our efforts. We argue about the nature of that world, and what might truly be an improvement. There is passion, ideology, information and technique. The offices where we practice are the laboratories where we execute our experiments. Academia is where we share them with our peers and students, those of the past and present, and speculate about those of the future.

Both practice and academia can be consuming and exhausting. Both at times can seem limited in reward. The work never seems to get as far as one hoped. Academia never adequately comes to grips with the full compliment of problems and

difficulties of practice. Together, however, they make a whole and inform each other, they fill in the yearned-for missing parts. Academia and practice when engaged fully form a dynamic intellectual and artistic flow of a constant (if at times painfully slow) feedback loop that advances the field. Many of the things one develops in the studio in school find their way into the field and can be seen a few years or a decade later in construction. Things being built and published then in turn drift into the schools and alter the conversation, influencing faculty and students alike.

In retrospect I note that nearly all of my teachers at the University of Washington had practices, and that we visited their work and critiqued it, sometimes harshly. They put their ideas and reputations out in public for all to see and evaluate. Some I admired. Some I disdained, but I did accord them respect for being in the world, for making the effort, and daring to be judged for it. When I entered the field many of the leaders in the profession of landscape architecture, both the past and present taught and practiced: Frederick Law Olmsted Jr; Charles Eliot; Garret Eckbo; Hideo Sasaki; Richard Haag; Ian McHarg; Peter Walker; and Kevin Lynch, for example, all did both. It seemed normal, desirable, and exemplary. It also turned out to take a lot of time. It necessitated offices and assistants of great ability, and often took a toll upon the lives of many associated with these individuals. Conversely, of course, there were a number of prominent practitioners I admire who didn't teach much at all: Beatrix Farrand; Daniel Kiley; Lawrence Halprin; Ed Stone Jr; and Robert Zion.

Today, as largely through the past century, the great majority of those who teach landscape architecture have practiced very little, often only a few years if that, before entering teaching. At times there seems to be an unfortunate gulf between academics and those who engage in the messy and often difficult life of practice, which can be particularly disappointing and rough in the first years after graduation. Like architecture, despite occasional shooting stars or the odd prodigy, it is not particularly a young person's game, at least not at the scale of many of our ambitions. For me the balance between working my way through a sequence of projects from student days in and around Rich Haag's office and several superb architects I apprenticed with and struggled under (the 10 years between 1961 and 1972) and the early decade with Bob Hanna and others teaching at Penn and building an office kept me optimistic and sane. I can't imagine how I would have done the things I've done if I hadn't kept one foot solidly in practice and the other firmly in academia.

**You have also borne witness to the major changes that have occurred at Penn and in the profession since the time of Ian McHarg. What do you think we have learned as a discipline and what do you think will be important for the future?**

Since I came to Penn in 1974 the world has changed and so have the profession and the department. The methods we helped to pioneer such as overlay and suitability mapping, ecological inventories and planning have become fairly standard procedures and are used around the world today and taught in one form or another at nearly all schools of landscape architecture. This combined with a concern for social purpose and culture in landscape design and planning that we began to explore at Penn in the 1970s and 80s, and subsequently that I pursued at Harvard, contributed to a shift in the focus of the department from natural factors as a theoretical agenda to that of culture in several manifestations.

After I returned in 1989 we brought John Dixon Hunt to Penn, and working with the young faculty—Dan Rose, Anu Mathur, James Corner, and Dana Tomlin—we reworked the curriculum. This coincided with a nationwide decline in regional planning and its funding in the Reagan years (which coincided with the dismantling of planning in Britain under Thatcher), which in turn further diminished

the physical presence of natural scientists within the department. Under JDH the faculty published significantly and due to his efforts a series of books on the history and theory of landscape architecture that now extends to over thirty has been published by the University of Pennsylvania Press. Again, as a result the tenor of discourse, papers, books, journals, and conferences in the field has altered and in part become more diverse, informed, and ambitious. Penn continued to set a course and change the field.

As this energy and activity rippled out from Philadelphia the department once more took stock and under the chairmanship of James Corner reflected upon what we should attend to that would continue to have a positive effect upon the field and society. Thus a number of us realized that the City was still something of a frontier for landscape architecture. It was a white blank on soils maps and not thought of as a landscape at all. Yet hundreds of millions of people around the world lived in cities and struggled with the quality of the environment and their lives. Agreeing with the observation of anthropologist Claude Levi Strauss that "the city is not an architectural problem, it is a cultural landscape", several of the faculty consciously shifted their concerns to urban areas and topics, launching a series of studios in a number of diverse settings around the world: in Asia, Europe, and Latin America, as well as across the US. Thus a concern for global issues of urban life and infrastructure informed by natural and cultural processes that operate on either a site or broader landscape scale has characterized the department for most of the past decade. As in the past, the effect upon teaching and practice elsewhere has been noticeable, with a number of peer institutions and colleagues now creating centers, curriculum, and professional literature and discourse, even debate focused upon urban landscape and its many issues.

This synopsis of past events may seem a bit Penn-centric, however, it seems accurate enough and possible to assert in retrospect and with some distance, but would not have been possible earlier at any one time while we were caught up in the activity and process of the work and events.

About the future, who knows? It is always both a bit hard to tell and a bit disheartening in the things that will almost certainly have to be dealt with, many of which are current problems that will persist to some degree. The biggest problems of the future are universal and synchronous, and they are related to health, resources, and the resilience of natural systems to sustain our ever-increasing urban population. Modern societies, led by the western example, whether democratic or authoritarian, tend to solve problems, or try to do so, through the use of large scale manipulation of science, technology, or projects—from agribusiness and monopolistic industrial practices to flood control and urban development. Such practices have created an entire new set of problems in almost every field of environment and social well-being.

Designers work incrementally, but at our best we attempt to conceive and shape our work in a manner that embraces broad systems and a holistic understanding of time and place. In physical terms cities are the result of thousands of competing individuals and forces continuously interacting. The challenge designers have faced time and again has been to find ways to leave a place (or city) richer than we find it, not diminished. At this moment in the early decades of the 21st century the central problem of nearly all urban design is the confrontation of increased scale and numbers. The question of building just and healthy cities when nearly every project threatens to remove or overwhelm aspects of the existing environment is universal while the answers are often individual and local.

When it comes to the future of practice, solutions, and trends however, it is good to remember that significant aspects of the future are almost always around in the present, but have not yet flowered into their full potential. One only has to think of small rodent-like mammals dashing about underfoot at the end of the great age of dinosaurs, or of the pre-digital age young folks playing about with computers at MIT, Cal Tech, and DARPA in the early 1970s when we were drawing with mechanical ink pens on overlain sheets of vellum and mylar, coloring maps on light tables, staring at stereo-pairs of aerial photographs, and sorting through 35 mm slides, in an attempt to marshal the material we needed to actually do our work. The future is already here, for better or worse, we just now have to live it wisely and well.

Nicholas Pevzner, M.L.A. '09

**As a teacher and editor of a new journal (scenario.com) you seem to be looking increasingly to work that is grounded in a more rigorous understanding of ecology. Could you briefly describe why you think this is important and how it relates to the recent history of the discipline?**

I'm interested in landscape that acts infrastructurally in the city. On the one hand, this means the organization of disjointed pieces of our increasingly complex urban fabric into a cohesive and legible framework. On the other, it means the literal support of essential urban functions—water quality protection, sewage treatment, energy supply, thermal regulation, and so on. While the first can be accomplished through the traditional design skill set, the second demands a more rigorous and technical level of engineering.

While the broad goals of landscape as infrastructure have entered the disciplinary conversation in both landscape practice and landscape education, the technical knowhow to deploy these landscape systems with fluency and control continues to be lacking. In practice, environmental engineers, ecologists, civil engineers and sustainability consultants can be brought onto the team for help with the specifics, but a heuristic understanding of the processes and feedbacks involved remains to be internalized.

If we are interested in positioning landscape not only as a boutique commodity or purely a space of leisure, but as a working part of the city that underlies and supports urban functioning, then we must better understand the impacts, uses, and services that an infrastructural landscape provides. This entails bringing more legibility not just to the elements that make up a city, but to the patterns and processes that take place in the urban environment. It also entails being much more precise in describing the goals of landscape as infrastructure, above and beyond its beauty or civic function. Our goal is to contribute to creating a better-performing city that is more efficient in its use of resources, healthier for its human inhabitants, and resilient to disruptions and disasters. To achieve this then ecology must be more than a metaphor for dynamic process in the urban landscape — we must incorporate it as a methodology that allows us to better describe the biophysical, geochemical, material, hydrological, and ecological interactions of urban systems, and to better calibrate both their individual and collective performance, in order to build a credible case for designed landscape infrastructures. We know that landscape has the potential to improve urban performance by providing ecosystem services (such as temperature regulation, microclimatic comfort, stormwater detention, water filtration, carbon sequestration, or even fuel supply), but unless these infrastructural functions can be implemented, tested, and replicated, they will remain secondary to the dominant civil engineering solutions.

At the same time, interest within the scientific community in constructed landscapes and in their potential to serve as green infrastructure is on the rise, but there are few channels of communication open between designers, ecologists, hydrologists, soil scientists, and environmental engineers. With Scenario Journal, based at Penn, my co-editor Steph Carlisle and I are trying to open a forum for critical exchange between these different disciplines.

## Chris Reed, M.L.A. '95

**There seems to be a clear lineage from Penn to your current practice. Is that how you see it?**

Penn was transformative for me. McHarg, Spirn, Corner, and Rose were all teaching at the time I started, and Ian's approach to designing and planning in concert with natural resources and systems was being both expanded and reformulated—challenged even—to better address social and urban issues. It was a ripe moment, the theory was deepening, the interdisciplinary discussions were robust; and the program continued to blossom as Mathur and Hunt joined the fray.

This expansive and critical work helped me reformulate my own ideas about what landscape is, and the roles it could play within the broader project of urbanism. Those interests continue to move my work—and clearly have enormously informed both the academy and practice today. How we continue to reinforce landscape as a cultural design project, and as a basis for how cities can be made or re-made to better address social needs and the very basics of food, water, and energy—these are among our challenges moving forward.

## Lucinda Sanders, M.L.A. '89

**Your vision of the future of the profession is that it needs to step up and play a greater leadership role in regard to some of the big issues facing the 21st century. How can we do this and what are some of the roles landscape architects could play in the future?**

Landscape architects have realized vitally important physical and intellectual projects over the last century and a half, which have dramatically and positively altered the way we live and the way we think about our surroundings. Over the duration of nearly a century, the profession has been defined by practice and academia and these two are often, but not consistently, in alignment. In practice, clients perpetuate the purview of landscape architects by providing opportunity, but always within limiting boundaries. Traditionally, those clients are defined as architects, urban designers, developers, institutions, political bodies, non-profits, and citizens with a relatively high net worth. These diverse client groups have defined the rather broad range of services landscape architects have been asked to provide. Beholden to the needs and motivations of these clients, the scope and ambition of practices are often only as strong and visionary as those who retain the services.

However, inside of practices where projects are undertaken within the confines of demands and constraints, ambitious landscape architects push boundaries when and where they can, helping to expand the reach and visibility of the profession. The significance of the brazen in the profession cannot be underestimated. They are the ones who have taken bold stances on particular beliefs, attitudes, and agendas. With these few prescient and impassioned individuals, who are unsurprisingly linked in some important way to the academic realm, the landscape architect's authority, impact and visibility have evolved slowly. This shift, earned through long and patient conversations—and downright persistence, has helped the profession gain trust among clients and respect from the public.

There is evidence of increased authority over the last two decades. Landscape architects are now leading large teams of consultants, engaging in complex and wide-reaching urban projects. They also are sitting as equals on teams holding significant and highly regarded positions. If the public is not cognizant of the authors—usually the heroic efforts of many individuals—of any landscape design, they are irresistibly drawn to spaces that are engaging, socially purposeful and poetic. That the profession has suffered less serious setbacks in the recession than our architect peers is an indication that landscape architecture is, in some circles, less likely to be perceived as a luxury commodity. The profession has grown in stature and visibility, but, given the current trajectory, will it continue to keep pace with 21st century issues, issues like those described in Jared Diamond's book "COLLAPSE—How Societies Choose to Fail or Succeed"?

The existing client base, while doing very important work, is presently serving a relatively narrow segment of our global society. There is no client base or planning or development model that presently recognizes landscape architects as viable contributors in territories that are in the greatest need of attention: coastal cities experiencing or vulnerable to devastation from sea level rise and flooding, cities with extreme densities and non-existent or fragile infrastructures, and regions with an unbalanced co-existence with ecosystem services, to name but a few. Very few leaders with power engage landscape architects as a 'go to group' to lead, organize, or even to participate, in formulating strategies to begin to tackle these crushing issues.

Yet, simultaneously, students in some landscape architecture programs, most notably at Penn, are routinely asked to think very deeply about precisely these topics. Historically, the academy is the place where questions have been explored and students are encouraged to provide speculative answers outside of the context and confines of a problem defined by the client. Landscape architecture at Penn has a tradition of being one of the institutions that simultaneously tackles the difficult and persistent questions free of a client base while also grounding students in history, theory, ecology and technology. This has been sound pedagogy.

Students leave the academy with an honest desire and a genuine commitment to use the agency of the design of the landscape to contribute to solving the bigger problems of the 21st century but are then greeted with narrow choices of employment and limited efficacy. The question then inevitably arises, is the academy doing enough to provide students with the necessary exposure to the development of implementable models that will enable them to effectively address these serious and life threatening challenges through the medium of the landscape and its adjacent systems? Not enough attention has been devoted to this emerging arena. Consequently, the gap widens between the pressing problems that students are asked to solve in the academy and those they are able to begin to solve once they depart the academy.

If landscape architects are to have more influential voices in these contemporary conversations, five vitally important shifts must occur, beginning in academia at Penn. First, students in landscape architecture need more exposure to the ways in which societal change occurs and they must be asked to imagine alternative models for implementation of their inspired and creative proposals. Secondly, emphasis must be on landscape architects becoming recognized participants in helping to solve the largest conundrum before us: how to create a culturally and spiritually fulfilling coexistence within the carrying capacity of the planet. Thirdly, landscape architecture students must be informed from day one that their professional label must not limit them. Fourth, know that we are deeply ensconced in the knowledge economy and that we are now entering an age of the

wisdom economy. Instead of just more knowledge, we must tap into the passions and state of mind that brought us to the profession in the first place in order to have those salient and transformational conversations about our future. And finally, there must be an active and open dialogue with students of landscape architecture about creating alternative platforms, other than practice, as we know it today, from which to operate.

For us to ask students to take on the challenge to raise the authority, visibility and impact of landscape architects in this new world, we must work with the students to help create new roles - advocacy, political, artistic, journalistic – that are respected and viable. We must first believe there are efficient new models from which to operate and then we must help to create those new forms of operation so that students know they can assume important roles toward building a sustainable future.

Meg Studer, M.L.A. '08

**You are interested in mapping complex systems, an area of research which is in part traceable back to Penn. Could you explain your current interests and how they align with a certain Penn legacy?**

I map two types of systems: landscape logistics and territorial projections. The former examines the maintenance operations and industrial ecologies—materials, labor, energy, and logistics coordination—underpinning urban infrastructure. The later explores the mass-media and computational construction of space, using the critical cartographies of post-war land-art as a filter to think through the territories projected by civil-defense planning and quantitative gaming.

Parallel to McHarg's interdisciplinary embrace of the physical and soft sciences, I work from a range of archives, geographic information systems, statistical and graphic software. Thus, while many of my technical tools borrow from his extensive overlay and tabular approach, my cartographic frameworks focus on intensively-articulated systems, combining the relational displays of social science—choropleths, treemaps, cartograms, isotypes—and the temporalized charts of landscape—phasing, timelines, scores. In the broadest sense, our mapping strategies are calibrated to locate 'sites' for intervention. Yet, unlike McHarg's "Design with Nature" (1969), my frame of reference is no longer climax ecology, default Keynesian implementation, or extensive, determinate geography. Rather, as in the 'region-making' of MVRDV or the writings of Keller Easterling, my maps visualize the mutually inflected political, economic, and ecological parameters producing space. I draw out design opportunities from the thresholds and nodes of on-going material and resource flows, the alliances between operational externalities and infrastructural (and institutional) inertia.

My treatments of space thus make me an heir to both James Corner's mapping agenda as well as da Cunha and Mathur's diagrammatic analysis. Their (now canonic)

insistence on hybrid parameters, adaptive human/non-human agents, the generative juxtaposition of systems and the creation of evocative explanations is clearly a precedent for my mapping practice. For me, additional mapping potential lies in cultivating a fluency in big-data. Always—already at the heart of modern governmental logic and the ideals of both planning and markets, the quantitative construction of territory needs to be critiqued, curated and cunningly wielded.

I hope to extend and evolve Corner and DaCunha/Mathur's mapping projects by situating the internal representation of complex systems in relation to shifting sensoria, subject construction, and distribution systems. My digital graphics and programming thus seek to develop an 'agency of mapping' that can be both rigorous and redundant, seductive and serial, visual and viral...

Lisa Switkin, M.L.A. '02

**As a Penn alum and member of James Corner Field Operations, what are your thoughts on the state of landscape architecture now?**

It is an exciting time when cities and towns are developing new strategies for the built environment by rethinking what it means to be green, sustainable, smart and livable. Architects, engineers and related disciplines are actively establishing special divisions in sustainable design to address this trend, but this is what we do as landscape architects, and it should be broadcast. It is inherent in our training and thinking and therefore landscape architects are poised to be leaders in this movement.

Landscape architecture is becoming more and more relevant with projects that respond to rapidly rising global issues such as contamination, water quality and management, land management, urban decay, the food and energy crisis, deforestation and large-scale ecological degradation. In addition, there is a wider recognition that quality open space and public realm can be a catalyst for economic development in addition to its other well known benefits of filtering air and water, cooling the environment, providing habitat for wildlife, contributing to carbon reduction targets, supporting expressions of civic engagement and improving physical health, well-being and quality of life.

I was introduced to 'systems thinking' at Penn. Understanding how built, natural, social, economic, and political systems influence one another and can be understood in the context of relationships with other systems is what makes Landscape architects ideal leaders for today's large-scale, complex urban design projects and design problems. We have a broad focus and are able to see the larger picture of how things fit together combined with design skills, attention to detail and a knack for navigating the process.

Now is our time. We are in a rare position to create value through the innovative repair, restoration and creation of urban landscapes. Penn should continue to train future leaders in systems thinking, to encourage creativity and innovation and to provide technical skills in the making and shaping of meaningful, imaginative, smart, productive and beautiful places.

Mark Thomann, M.L.A. '99

**In your studios you are challenging conventional design methods. Could you explain your aims?**

My studios challenge a linear design approach and are structured as experimental design inquiries into the seemingly chaotic patterns of modern life. Each of my studio projects investigates methods to sort, edit and weave endless streams of data and influence into design strategies, patterns and relationships. The approach is multidisciplinary; students are required to step outside of the traditional confines of the 'designer's world' to absorb as much of the web of life as possible through immersion, exploration and exposure to a variety of influences in order to frame their design.

The goal of my projects is design informed - and continually transformed - by investigations and experiences of the complex relationships among natural phenomena, inter-social dynamics, and ecosystems. Ecosystems are not isolated from each other, but are interrelated. The first principle of ecology is that every living organism has an ongoing and continual relationship with every other element that makes up its environment. The ecosystem is composed of two entities: the entirety of life (the biocoenosis) and the medium in which life exists (the biotope).

Like the weather, design is inseparable from personal experience and external influences. As we move towards the assimilation of work/play and architecture/nature, designers must develop tools to negotiate complex assemblages of influence, social ecologies, systems, data sets, patterns, and behaviors, which are constantly shifting and changing and evolving. I am pushing the boundaries of linear design to create what I call dynamic design, which, like the weather, social interactions, and ecosystems are defined by changeability, mutability and the potential to evolve.

Of course without some kind of human construct in the designer's mind there would be chaos. My answer to this problem is the creative application of algorithms to embed ideas and experience into an emerging future. The algorithm is a dynamic and intuitive process. By applying an algorithm we create a heuristic set of rules and flexible procedures for discovery and decision making. The creativity of the process lies in playing out the formula and seeing the project evolve, adapt and transform according to the changing variables and collaboration of the players involved. New relationships, ideas and questions emerge from the every small tweak of the variables and through the human social interaction inherent in the approach.

Dana Tomlin

**Somewhat off to one side you have been working assiduously on GIS algorithms. Could you speak briefly about your research and why it is important to the larger landscape architectural enterprise in the 21st century?**

As a high school student trying to decide how to spend the rest of my life, I found there was something about architecture and something (very different) about forestry that had always held the greatest interest. Now decades later, I find that these interests are just as strong as ever; and not only have I managed to satisfy them, I have also been able to get paid now and then for doing so. The trick has been to forego each in favor of pursuing something in between. Having initially made the decision head toward forestry, it was the dean of the school I was about to attend who first opened my eyes to landscape architecture and thereby compelled me to leave that school not long after I arrived. Over the next several years, I would go back and forth between the academic worlds of (not just architecture or landscape architecture per se but, more generally) environmental design and (not just forestry per se but, more generally) environmental planning.

It was from somewhere between those worlds that there emerged this thing called 'GIS,' geographic information systems.  Still in the days when cards had to be punched and submitted to computers that occupied whole buildings, it was all very mysterious, intimidating, and (to my eyes at least as a budding young artsy-fartsy designer) antithetical to the essential nature and purpose of creativity. That changed, however, when I was challenged one day by a clever professor to try to get that machine to read a map. Surely a computer should be smart enough to be able to see what I see. Distances, directions, sizes, shapes - all just a matter of straightforward geometrical measurement.  But what about making decisions? Optimization, allocation, planning, design...The prospect of being able to use that machine not only to describe 'what is' but also to envision 'what could be' and

ultimately to prescribe 'what should be' was at once both elusive and seductive. It was seductive enough in fact to lure me into a doctoral program (at a forestry school) and a teaching position (at a design school) where I could explore the prospect in a manner that has, since then, always felt more like a hobby than a profession.

A large part of the reason for this has been timing. Even today, I still manage to ride a wave of ever-increasing interest and improvement in modern digital technology.  hat wave initially drew its strength from things like personal computers and graphical use interfaces but then drew even more from equipment that could be relied upon to get smaller, more powerful and less expensive with each passing year. This continued with the advent of the Internet, global positioning systems, mobile devices, and routine use of the technology by, well, almost everyone.

My own opportunity to ride that wave has largely been due to interests that are oriented as much or more toward the development of GIS as toward the use of this tool in any one area of practical application. What started as favors for classmates seeking specialized GIS capabilities would eventually result in the development of a software package (the world's most widely used of its kind at

the time, perhaps because it was distributed for free), a doctoral dissertation, plenty of publications, and lots opportunities to put my ideas to work. In short, those ideas revolved around a computational language that has come to be referred to as 'Map Algebra'. Whereas a conventional algebra might use elementary mathematical operations to add, subtract, multiply, or divide numbers, 'Map Algebra' uses elementary cartographic operations to superimpose maps onto another, to measure distances, determine directions, calculate travel times, characterize shapes, compute slopes, generate viewsheds, simulate flow patterns, determine paths of minimum cost, and so on. Variations on this methodology are evident in virtually all of today's raster-based (i.e. image- rather than drawing-oriented) geographic information systems.

But what about satisfying those early interests in architecture and forestry? While the use of GIS has now been embraced by both of those fields and many others in between, how does the design of geospatial algorithms relate to the design of geographical space? In short, the answer is 'directly.' Those who tend to favor the right-hand side of the brain know full well that the ability and the inclination to cast all sorts of problems in geometric terms is not only strangely empowering but strangely enjoyable as well. And many of those who design computer software know the same is true for problems whose 'spatial' dimensions are more logical than physical in nature. For me, the opportunity to choreograph processes and generate patterns in the virtual world(s) of GIS has been no less challenging, satisfying, or consequential than doing so in that other world just outside.

Jerry van Eyck

**Do you feel that in the last few decades things have improved for practicing landscape architecture. If so why? You have always been involved with leading firms—where are you trying to take your own practice now?**

Landscape architecture is one of the most dynamic, most diverse, broadest in scope, and holistic design disciplines around.

Every new project is a unique situation that involves defining a set of challenges and creating a new approach each time. There should be no rule or formula for landscape architecture, however, some tenets may help people categorize and understand the trends and enrichment of our profession over time.

It is the landscape architect's role to relate to context, as well as to create context: context for living, context for work, context for play, and context for transit. In an effort to make places large and small, it is a landscape architects role to contemplate the interaction of user and context.

The creation of a contextual place also effects people's emotions. Whether they are places of entertainment, places of relaxation, places for consumption, or places to call home, how people interact with environments can range from the sheer poetic to the ultra commercial. In making places that are durable, we strive to create not just environmental sustainability, but also social and economic sustainability.

Every young graduate landscape designer will experience that landscape architecture is about people and especially about anticipation. And therein lies perhaps the biggest dissimilarity with what he or she was taught while roaming in academia. Landscape architecture is more than mastering a vernacular or a set of skills. It is more than being capable of generating design concepts based on analysis and research. It is also more than knowing how to construct a site and every detail in it.

Creativity can't flourish in a vacuum. A design is shaped by conditions and constraints. By the goals and wishes of a client, by politics, by budget restrictions, by location, by availability of materials, and by the limitations of the contractor.

As educators, it is our duty to prepare our students to become young professionals who understand that at the moment they enter the world of practicing Landscape architecture the actual learning is yet to begin. To practice Landscape architecture is to be a perpetual student, to learn over and over, with every project.

With each new project we discover what it means when a project (finally) 'works'. Our projects may be minimalistic, frivolous, high-tech, organic, rich, or simplistic. Perhaps we still may preach of ecology or cultural history in a semi religious way, but we continue to learn from every project, and each time we will find out that we cannot predict a project's outcome. We need to habitually re-invent ourselves, and with this we will also, constantly, re-invent our profession.

## Charles Waldheim

**Now chair at Harvard, could you reflect on your education at Penn?**

At Penn as a Master of Architecture candidate in the Graduate School of Fine Arts, I first understood that the design disciplines could share intellectual commitments and objects of study. I learned that the design disciplines share significant intellectual and institutional histories. Equally, I learned that the challenges of the contemporary city often resist easy professional or disciplinary boundaries.

My own intellectual project and desire to describe and intervene upon the contemporary city was first formulated at Penn. This was informed by the intellectual milieu at Penn and the work of my mentors and colleagues in the

School including Mohsen Mostafavi, David Leatherbarrow, Homa Farjadi, and James Corner, among many other influences. It was at Penn that I first appreciated intellectual and academic leadership. While at Penn, I benefited from the service and vision of two extraordinary individuals in leadership roles, Adele Santos, then chair of the department of architecture, and Anne Spirn, then chair of the department of landscape architecture. The milieu that I was immersed in for graduate work was shaped, as much as anything, by faculty appointments made during their terms.

Of course, Harvard GSD and Penn GSFA share a mutually beneficial, and long-standing set of conversations and commitments. Neither institution could be completely described without mention of the other. Of course that communication has informed both institutions and continues in various forms to this day.

While my experience in the Master of Architecture at Penn exposed me to landscape as a medium of contemporary urbanism, it was in the department of landscape architecture at Penn that I found the disciplinary and intellectual grounding for my own aspirations. That would not have been possible without the deep and profound impact on Penn made by Holmes Perkins, Laurie Olin, Ian

McHarg, and a range of Harvard affiliates over many years. My own professional arc, having taken me to the Harvard GSD, is unimaginable absent the long-standing intellectual and disciplinary commitments of PennDesign. Of course, this is an ongoing conversation, so, to be continued...

## Sally Willig

**Why do you think it is important that we learn to read the land around us and how do you open students eyes to this?**

Sensitive thoughtful design and wise land use decision-making that protects humans and the environment require an ecological approach to site analysis that evaluates abiotic and biotic factors and determines key linking processes. The Philadelphia region provides an ideal setting for learning to 'read the landscape' as the climate and geology change in moving from the New Jersey barrier islands northwest to the Appalachian Mountains of Pennsylvania. Associated changes in topography, soils, vegetation, wildlife, and disturbance, natural and human-caused, become clear in exploring, characterizing, and comparing natural areas along this transect. Students learn best when their senses are fully engaged as occurs, for example, on our kayak trips down the Batsto River in the Pine Barrens of New Jersey in the early fall. On glorious warm days they see the quartz sand substrate and experience the rise and fall of the terrain and accompanying variation in soil moisture and vegetation. They hear the wind in the pitch pine and the crashing of boats into shrub-lined riverbanks mixed with laughter. They can smell the spicy scent of crushed sweetbay magnolia leaves and feel the soft muck in the Atlantic white cedar swamp. They can even taste the tart cranberry in the savanna, an artifact of historic bog iron mining, brimming with diverse herbaceous plants including the intriguing carnivores. In immersing themselves in and moving through a landscape, the students come to understand in a very visceral way the interrelationship of site factors. Every site from the degraded tidal waterfront to the more natural mountain ridge during fall raptor migration has a story to tell. Consideration of processes enables students to unlock the narratives and develop a greater understanding and appreciation of different landscapes. The ecological approach to unraveling a site's history will guide students as they develop as designers and move forward into practice.

the perfect fit. Finally, the field of landscape architecture seemed like a great choice for a career. The scientific approach that was lacking in school became de rigueur, so I welcomed and embraced it. At the time I went to my 15-year reunion, I was on television, radio, and several print media for my work restoring landfills; it was kind of a repudiation of tough days as an undergrad.

I am highly motivated by the desire to improve the earth upon which we live, and to help make it sustainable for all generations to come.

## Bill Young

**You seem to have a great love for what you do. What motivates you as a practitioner and a teacher?**

I teach because it is a chance to share knowledge and wisdom; I teach because it may inspire a student; I teach because it is so rewarding; I teach because I have something to share.

When I went to SUNY Forestry to study landscape architecture, I was a decent student. But my best classes were outside the LA curriculum. I preferred classes with real learning and rigor. Studio was abstract and arbitrary. So, years later, when the industry embraced ecology and the environmental sciences, my career blossomed. My motivation was always there, but now my practice seemed like

# Image Credits

## Cover
Image one: L.B. Ambler, Jr. (1931). "A country estate". University of Pennsylvania Bulletin.

Image two: The Architectural Archives of the University of Pennsylvania. (Col. 122).

Image three: James Corner. (1996). "Pedalogical Drift". Taking Measures Across the American Landscape.

## Front Endpaper
Photo by Barrett Doherty. (2013).

## Page 4
Photo by Barrett Doherty. (2013).

## Page 12
Image one: Carol McHarg Collection. (2013).

Image two: Anne Whiston Spirn Collection. (2013).

## Page 13
Image one: Photo by Patrick McMullen. (2013).

Image two: National Endowment for the Arts Collection. (2013).

## Pages 14-15
Photo by Barrett Doherty. (2013).

## Pages 18-19
(1915). "University Library (built 1890, Furness, Evans & Co., architect; now Anne and Jerome Fisher Fine Arts Library) and College Hall College Hall (built 1871-1872, Thomas Webb Richards, architect), exterior." The University Archives of the University of Pennsylvania.

## Page 20
(1914). University of Pennsylvania Bulletin.

## Page 21
Image one: Harris & Ewing. (1914). "George Burnap. Landscape Architect." Library of Congress Prints and Photographs Division.

Image two: Yousuf Karsh. "Portrait of Jacques Gréber." Library and Archives Canada.

## Pages 24-25
E, Moebius. (1907). "College Hall (built 1871-1872, Thomas Webb Richards, architect), interior, drafting room (310)." The University Archives of the University of Pennsylvania.

## Page 26
(1924). University of Pennsylvania Bulletin.

## Page 27
(1924). University of Pennsylvania Bulletin.

## Page 29
(1933). Student transcript. The Architectural Archives of the University of Pennsylvania.

## Page 30
Image one: L.B. Ambler, Jr. (1931). "A residential subdivision". University of Pennsylvania Bulletin.

Image two: L.B. Ambler, Jr. (1931). "A country estate". University of Pennsylvania Bulletin.

## Page 31
Image one: M.S. Wehrly. (1933). "A hillside estate in California". University of Pennsylvania Bulletin.

Image two: Alfred Edwards. (1933). "A preparatory school." University of Pennsylvania Bulletin.

## Pages 34-35
James L. Dillon. (1906). "Hayden Hall (built 1895 as the School of Dentistry, Edgar V. Seeler, architect), exterior." The University Archives of the University of Pennsylvania.

## Page 36
Oliver M. Fanning. (1934). "A city park". University of Pennsylvania Bulletin.

## Page 37
Image one: Joe Walter Langran. (1935). "A suburban development". University of Pennsylvania Bulletin.

Image two: Joe Walter Langran. (1937). "A low-rent housing project". University of Pennsylvania Bulletin.

## Page 38
Maurice F Plotkins. (1938). "A plan for a park. University of Pennsylvania Bulletin.

## Page 39
Image one: (1939). University of Pennsylvania Bulletin.

Image two: (1939). University of Pennsylvania Bulletin.

## Pages 40-41
Student transcripts. The Architectural Archives of the University of Pennsylvania.

## Pages 44-45
(1942). "World War II, ROTC students training in fox holes behind University Museum." The University Archives of the University of Pennsylvania.

## Page 46
(1935). "G. Holmes Perkins (1904-2004), A.M. (hon.) 1971, L.L.D. (hon.) 1972, portrait photograph." The University Archives of the University of Pennsylvania.

## Page 47
(1951). University of Pennsylvania Bulletin.

## Page 48
(1952). University of Pennsylvania Bulletin.

## Page 49
The Architectural Archives of the University of Pennsylvania. (Col. 109), by the gift of Ian L. McHarg.

## Pages 52-53
William H. Rau. (1898). "University Library (built 1890, Furness, Evans & Co., architect; now Anne and Jerome Fisher Fine Arts Library), interior, reading room, semi-aerial photograph." The University Archives of the University of Pennsylvania.

## Page 55
The Architectural Archives of the University of Pennsylvania. (Col. 122).

## Page 56
(1957). University of Pennsylvania Bulletin.

## Page 57
(1958). University of Pennsylvania Bulletin.

## Pages 58-59
The Architectural Archives of the University of Pennsylvania. (Col. 054)

## Page 60
Jules Schick. (1958). "Graduate School of Fine Arts, studio discussion." The University Archives of the University of Pennsylvania.

## Pages 64-65
"Fine Arts Building (architects rendering)". The University Archives of the University of Pennsylvania.

## Page 67
(1964). "Student protest, against the building of Meyerson Hall." The University Archives of the University of Pennsylvania.

**Pages 68-69**
WRT collection. (2013)

**Page 70**
(1965). University of Pennsylvania Bulletin.

**Page 71**
The Architectural Archives of the University of Pennsylvania. (Col. 109), by the gift of Ian L. McHarg.

**Pages 72-73**
The Architectural Archives of the University of Pennsylvania. (Col. 122).

**Pages 74-75**
The Architectural Archives of the University of Pennsylvania. (Col. 122).

**Pages 76-77**
The Architectural Archives of the University of Pennsylvania. (Col. 122).

**Pages 78-79**
The Architectural Archives of the University of Pennsylvania. (Col. 122).

**Pages 80-81**
The Architectural Archives of the University of Pennsylvania. (Col. 122).

**Page 83**
The Architectural Archives of the University of Pennsylvania. (Col. 109), by the gift of Ian L. McHarg.

**Pages 84-85**
(1970). Retrieved from www.earthweek1970.org.

**Page 86**
The Architectural Archives of the University of Pennsylvania. (Col.024). Photo by Becky Young.

**Page 87**
The Architectural Archives of the University of Pennsylvania. (Col.024), by the gift of Sir Peter Shepheard.

**Page 88**
Carol McHarg Collection. (2013)

**Page 89**
Laurie Olin Collection. (2013)

**Pages 90-91**
The Architectural Archives of the University of Pennsylvania. (Col. 109), by the gift of Ian L. McHarg.

**Page 92**
The Architectural Archives of the University of Pennsylvania. (Col.109). Photo by Becky Young.

**Pages 100-101**
The Architectural Archives of the University of Pennsylvania. (Col.024), by the gift of Sir Peter Shepheard.

**Pages 102-103**
The Architectural Archives of the University of Pennsylvania. (Col. 122).

**Pages 104-105**
Andropogon Collection. (2013)

**Page 106**
OLIN collection. (2013)

**Page 107**
Image one: © Peter Mauss/Esto. All rights reserved.

Image two: Sahar Coston-Hardy. OLIN collection. (2013)

**Page 108**
(1975). "College Green (Blanche P. Levy Park) in the snow." The University Archives of the University of Pennsylvania.

**Page 109**
The Architectural Archives of the University of Pennsylvania. (Col.024), by the gift of Sir Peter Shepheard.

**Page 110**
Lucinda Reed Sanders. (1979). "Fitler Square".

**Page 111**
Image one: Ed Hollander. (1983). "Jacobsburg Cluster Housing". Penn and Ink.

Image two: Alice Richardson. (1983). "The Horse Farm". Penn and Ink.

**Pages 112-113**
Ed Hollander. (1983). "Pennypack Wildlife Refuge". Penn and Ink.

**Pages 116-117**
Photo by Barrett Doherty. (2013).

**Page 119**
Penn and Ink. (1984).

**Page 120**
Niall Kirkwood. (1985). "Gorgas Park Restoration." Penn and Ink.

**Page 121**
James Corner. (1986). "City Vision for a Metropolitan Philadelphia".

**Page 122**
Penn and Ink. (1994).

**Page 131**
Image one: (1984) New York: Basic Books.

Image two: (1998). Yale University Press.

**Page 134**
Alan Berger. (1988).

**Page 135**
Anuradha Mathur. (1990). "Winterthur Garden and Estate".

**Page 136**
Anne Whiston Spirn Collection. (2013)

**Page 137**
The Architectural Archives of the University of Pennsylvania. (Col.014), by the gift of Lawrence Halprin.

**Pages 138-139**
Anne Whiston Spirn. (1991). "West Philadelphia Landscape Project".

**Pages 142-143**
Photo by Barrett Doherty. (2013).

**Page 144**
Photo by Barrett Doherty. (2013).

**Page 146**
Image one: (2004) University of Pennsylvania Press.

Image two: (2012) Reaktion Books.

**Pages 148-149**
Eric Husta and Steven Sattler. (1996).

**Page 151**
Image one: Jonathan Reo. (1997).

Image two: Charles Neer, Eliza Booth, Mark Meagher, Landscape Drawing. (1997).

**Pages 152-153**
Patricia Uribe. (1999).

**Page 154**
James Corner + Stan Allen. (1999) "Downsview Park, Toronto: Emergence Through Adaptive Management".

**Page 155**
James Corner Field Operations. (2001) "Freshkills Park, 2030".

**Page 156**
Photo by Barrett Doherty. (2013).

**Page 161**
Image one: James Corner. (1996). "Pivot Irrigators, CA". Taking Measures Across the American Landscape.

Image two: James Corner. (1996). "Pueblo Bonito, NM". Taking Measures Across the American Landscape.

**Page 164**
Image one: Anuradha Mathur and Dilip da Cuhna. (2001). "Crevassing Levees". Mississippi Floods: Designing a Shifting Landscape.

Image two: Anuradha Mathur and Dilip da Cuhna. (2001). "Engineered Curves". Mississippi Floods: Designing a Shifting Landscape.

**Page 165**
Photo by Barrett Doherty. (2013).

**Page 166**
Shian-Po Liao. (2001).

**Page 167**
Chih-Ciun (Grace) Ling. (2001).

**Page 168**
Ellen Neises. (2002).

**Page 169**
Michael Steiner. (2002).

**Pages 172-173**
Photo by Barrett Doherty. (2013).

**Pages 174-175**
Shannon Scovell. (2008) "Living Grid Park - MAC Central Open Space."

**Pages 176-177**
Youngjoon Choi. (2008). "Living Pixel".

**Page 178**
Rebecca Fuchs, Keya Kunte, and Kimberly Cooper. (2008). "Seeding Stability: A Strategy for Relocation and Reorganization in a Medellin Barrio".

**Page 179**
Nantawan Sirisup. (2008).

**Page 180**
James Corner Field Operations. (2009).

**Page 181**
Photo by Barrett Doherty. (2013).

**Page 182**
Johanna Barthmaier. (2009).

**Page 183**
Emily Vogler. (2009).

**Page 184**
Marisa Bernstein. (2011).

**Page 185**
Alejandro Vazquez. (2011).

**Pages 186-187**
Johanna Barthmaier. (2011) "Tempelhof Wasserpark".

**Pages 188-189**
Meghan Storm. (2012) "Off the Reservation:A Seed for Change".

**Pages 190-191**
Photos by Barrett Doherty. (2013).

**Page 192**
Photos by Barrett Doherty. (2013).

**Pages 196-197**
Claire Hoch (2013).

**Pages 208-246**
All images provided by individuals as listed, with the exception of Charles Waldheim, photo by Sienna Scarff Design.

**Rear Endpaper**
Photo by Barret Doherty. (2013).